Legends of Oakland Plantation

The Prud'hommes of Natchitoches Parish

Revised Edition

By Sandra Prud'homme Haynie

Edited by Mary Breazeale Cunningham

Haynie
LaPressCo Printing
Shreveport, Louisiana
2002

First Published 2001
Copyright©Sandra Prud'homme Haynie 2001
First Edition ISBN 0-9714260-0-7
Revised Edition ISBN 0-9714260-1-5
2002
Published by Sandra Prud'homme Haynie
Shreveport, Louisiana
Printed by LaPressCo Printing
Shreveport, LA

2nd Edition

TABLE OF CONTENTS

ACKNOWLEDGMENTS

It is difficult to properly thank the scores of friends, relatives and strangers that assisted me with this publication. My husband's patience and encouragement were overwhelming. My children and stepchildren graciously shared the family computer with me. Cousins I hadn't seen for years opened their homes, hearts and scrapbooks as we diligently searched for photos and clues of the past. During this quest I met some cousins for the very first time yet, the bond was immediate and precious. Those who were once strangers are now friends. To all of you, I say thanks.

In actuality it would be impossible to list each and everyone that assisted me. However, I would especially like to thank my immediate family and my editor, Mary "Cissy" Cunningham, as well as, those who shared photographs and documents whose names will not be repeated but are listed in the text. In addition, I thank the following; the Kenneth Prud'homme family, the Ted Duggan family, the Mayo Prud'homme family, Eric Brock, Alicia Cunningham, Elise Cloutier, Giles Robbins, Henry Baker, Edmund Thomas, Dana Tarrant, Dan Willard, Penny Nowell Brown, Mary Linn Wernet, Stephen Hatton, Sonny Carter, Dominica Carrierre, Laura Soulliere, Carla Cowles, Elizabeth Russell, Bob Stark, Tracy Burch, Gordon Rountree, Gayle Hamilton and Theodosia Nolan.

Dedicated to my husband, Mike, my children, Dylan and Scott, my stepchildren, Marshall, Caroline and Clare and to my grandmother, Lucile "Lu Lu" Keator Prud'homme, for without her diligence, much of Oakland's history would have faded into obscurity.

2

INTRODUCTION

I always considered myself quite fortunate to have grown up on a farm. I never thought our farm to be of historical significance until I was an adult. My grandparents, James Alphonse and Lucile Prud'homme, just happened to live in the Big House at Oakland Plantation and we lived down the road. My father and uncle farmed the land.

My family had lived in the Big House since it was built in 1821. Prior to that my ancestors lived on the land in smaller homes until my great-great-great-great grandfather, Jean Pierre Emmanuel Prud'homme (hereinafter referred to as "Emmanuel"), made a success of growing cotton and built the Big House. Oakland is one of only two plantations west of the Mississippi that was farmed by the same family for over two hundred years. In 1988 it was formally recognized as a Bicentennial Farm. We were farmers. My father's family had always farmed and that's just the way it was.

In the 1980s I heard the family talk about how our cousin, Robert "Bobby" DeBlieux, had approached my grandfather about selling Oakland to the government and making it a national park. Initially, I, not unlike the rest of my family, thought Bobby had lost his mind. The plantation had always been in the family and we would never sell the plantation to anyone outside the family. Well, after several years of deliberation we finally realized that our cousin had not lost his mind but actually had envisioned a wonderful plan. After drying our tears we did indeed sell our beloved Oakland to the Department of the Interior in 1997. Oakland became part of the Cane River Creole National Historical Park.

Oakland Plantation is about a family, a very large extended Creole family. Many scholars have tried to define the word "Creole." Some refer to Creoles as the aristocratic people of European descent who were born in America. Others claim the term was used to distinguish Louisiana's French from the Anglo-Americans. Later the French-

Africans were referred to as Creoles of Color. Undoubtedly over the years the term has evolved resulting in multiple broad definitions. This writer will not attempt to define the term but only to emphasize that the "Creole" culture is separate and distinct from the "Cajun" culture of South Louisiana.

Most of what is written in the pages that follow consists of my memories and the stories passed on to me by my relatives. My most influential historian was my grandmother, Lucile Keator Prud'homme, affectionately known by those who loved her as "Lu Lu." While most of what is written is based on folklore I have attempted to verify these stories by spending countless hours researching archives, libraries, courthouses and genealogy records. The purpose of this work is not to specifically document each and every event that occurred at the plantation but to present vignettes about the people of Oakland Plantation. I have provided my sources for those who seek further information. My intention is to preserve the memories of Oakland when it was a home…a home… and not just a national park.

Prud'homme coat of arms

Oakland Plantation, Bermuda, Natchitoches Parish, Louisiana

HISTORY OF OAKLAND

Long before the American Revolution, the riots in Paris and the fall of the Bastille, a Frenchman, Jean Pierre Philippe Prud'homme, was actively pursuing his dreams in the New World, the territory of Louisiana. At the time of the French Revolution (1789-1799) the former Frenchman Jean Pierre Philippe Prud'homme and his son, Jean Baptiste Prud'homme, were both deceased after having established themselves as *inhabitants* in the Louisiana territory. During the 100 year period from 1718-1818 the Prud'hommes had established themselves in Louisiana before the Big House at Oakland Plantation was even built.

In 1803, about the time Lewis and Clark began their expedition west, Emmanuel Prud'homme, a third generation Prud'homme of Louisiana, was perfecting his skill of growing cotton. The Creole gentleman was successful.

The Big House at Oakland Plantation, in central Louisiana near the community of Natchitoches, was built by slave labor for Emmanuel Prud'homme and his wife, Catherine Lambre, in 1821. Initially the plantation was not named Oakland. It was known as Bermuda or Prud'homme Plantation. Herein, it will be referred to as Oakland for the sake of simplicity.

Jean Pierre Emmanuel Prud'homme (1762-1845)

JEAN PIERRE PHILIPPE PRUD'HOMME
(CIRCA 1673-1739)

Emmanuel's grandfather, Jean Pierre Philippe Prud'homme, was a native of Roman, Dauphine, France. He was born about 1673 and came to Louisiana as a soldier in the French army during the early 1700s. Emmanuel's grandmother, Marie Catherine Messelier Picard, found her way to the new country via a different route, for she was a casket girl. It appears she made her voyage to the New World at the age of 14 years aboard *La Baleine* in 1719.[1]

From the moment the French frontiersmen began settling in Louisiana there was a cry for French wives. Several shiploads of women ranging in quality from hoydens to proper ladies took the voyage. The Company of the Indies sponsored several of these voyages by providing the girls with a dowry and traveling expenses to the New World. The girls were called casket girls because their belongings were stored in small trunks called *cassettes* (English interpretation, casket.)[2]

---

[1] It is difficult to determine how Marie Catherine Messelier Picard arrived in the New World. Sources reveal she may have been a young pauper housed in *La Salpetriere*, the female section of the *Hopital General* in Paris. Conrad, Glenn R. A Dictionary of Louisiana Biography, The Louisiana Historical Association in cooperation with The Center for Louisiana Studies of the University of Southwestern Louisiana, New Orleans 1988. Legend reveals her father, Joseph Picard, lived in New Orleans.

[2] It does not appear that Marie Catherine made the voyage with the Ursuline Nuns' casket girls as they did not reach New Orleans until 1727. De Villiers du Terrage, Marc. The Last Years of French Louisiana, Center for Louisiana Studies, USL, Lafayette, La. 1982

Marie Catherine may have left Paris as a pauper hoping for a better life. She may have been one of the more fortunate girls with her dowry in a portable hope chest including two dresses, two petticoats, six headdresses and sundries. Nonetheless she started her journey hoping to find a proper husband and knowing she would probably never see her homeland again.

Jean Pierre Philippe Prud'homme made his home in the settlement of Natchitoches established by Louis Juchereau de St. Denis in 1714. Jean Pierre Philippe began his life in the New World as a French soldier but later pursued the profession of a merchant and trader. It was during one of his trips to New Orleans as a trader that he met his future bride. Marie Catherine was reputed to be very lovely.

At the time of Jean Pierre Philippe and Marie Catherine's marriage France controlled the Louisiana territory. They made a home at the French fort in Natchitoches and had eight children, one of whom was Jean Baptiste Prud'homme.

Fort St. Jean Baptiste (replica, Natchitoches, La.)

JEAN BAPTISTE PRUD'HOMME
(1735-1786)

Jean Baptiste was born at the French fort in 1735 and was educated to be a physician. He was a court physician to the King of France, *Docteur de Roi*. He later returned to the French military post, Fort Jean Baptiste in Natchitoches, where he continued his profession as a physician. While in Natchitoches he practiced under the tutelage of the surgeon-major Daniel Pain. He opened a hospital in Natchitoches at the southwest corner of Jefferson and Touline in Natchitoches. This building was later converted to the Inn Hotel. In 1758, Jean Baptiste bought nine arpents of land with money he had inherited from his godfather. Legend reveals his family received a land grant from the French government.

Jean Baptiste's first wife, Marie Francoise Chevert, and infant son died in 1757. His second wife was from Natchez, Mississippi. Jean Baptiste Prud'homme and his second wife, Marie Josephine Charlotte Henriette Collantin, had eight children. Emmanuel was the third child born of this union.

In 1763, after Spain gained control of Louisiana, Jean Baptiste retired from medicine and began developing his land. He was quite successful as a planter. One of his sons, Emmanuel, began farming 700 acres in the 1780s on both sides of the Red River about 13 miles south of the settlement of Natchitoches. Emmanuel purchased this same land about 1795. A small family home was built on this land close to the river.

France regained Louisiana from Charles III of Spain during the turn of the century, but not for long. In 1803 Napoleon sold Louisiana to the United States. The United States government was skeptical of the large land grants established during the time of French and Spanish ownership of the territory. Emmanuel would later have to prove his claim in ownership of this land to the satisfaction of the United States' authorities.

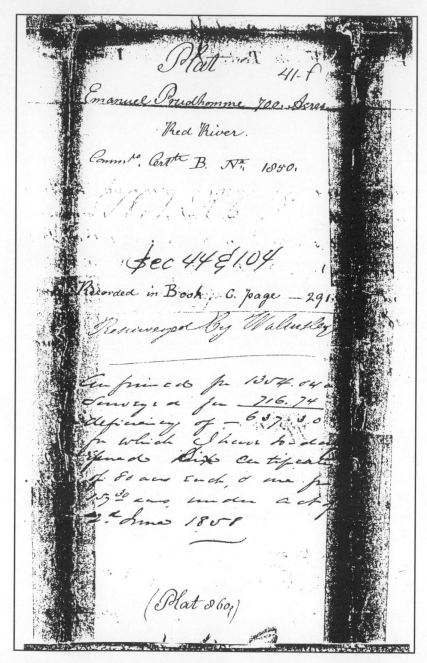

Plat of land: Emmanuel's claim validating ownership. Note adjacent land belonging to his brother, Antoine Prud'homme, and brother-in-law, Remy Lambre Courtesy Louisiana State Land Office, Baton Rouge, Louisiana and David Williamson

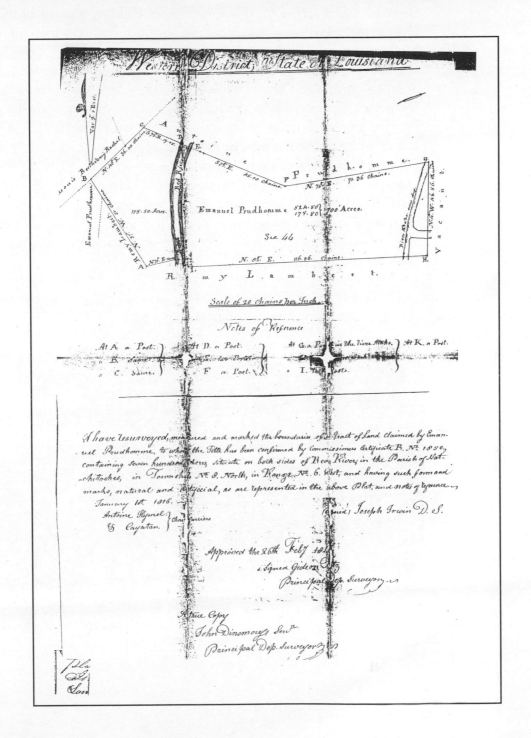

Some of Jean Baptiste Prud'homme's other children also established plantations. His son, Antoine Prud'homme who was married to Marie Jacques Lambre resided on a plantation adjacent to Emmanuel's. By the early 1900s Antoine's plantation home fell into disrepair and was dismantled, circa 1915. His daughter, Anna "Nanette", married Philippe Guillaume (William) Benjamin Giles Duparc and resided on a plantation in St. James Parish currently known as Laura Plantation. His daughter, Marie Louise, married Jean Francois Rouquier and they resided in Natchitoches in the home now known as the Prud'homme-Rouquier Home. His daughter, Suzanne married Remy Lambre whose plantation was also adjacent to Emmanuel's on the opposite side. Two of Jean Baptiste's sons, Baptiste and Francois, died as infants and another, Dominique, left home never to be heard from again.

It is interesting to note that three of Jean Baptist Prud'homme's children married three of Jacques Lambre's children.

Prud'homme-Rouquier Home, home of Marie Louise Prud'homme Rouquier, sister of Emmanuel Prud'homme. Currently owned by the Service League of Natchitoches

Nanette Prud'homme Duparc (1768-1862) sister of Emmanuel Prud'homme, age 82, photo taken at Duparc Plantation circa 1850. Courtesy Norman and Sand Marmillion of Laura Plantation

Duparc Plantation (Laura Plantation, Vacherie, Louisiana) Courtesy Norman and Sand Marmillion of Laura Plantation

*Antoine Prud'homme
(1764-1856), brother of
Emmanuel Prud'homme.
Courtesy Robert "Bobby"DeBlieux*

*Madame Antoine Prud'homme,
nee Marie Jacques Lambre
(1775-1855)
Courtesy Robert "Bobby"DeBlieux*

Jean Pierre Emmanuel Prud'homme (1762-1845) Portrait painted in Paris, 1822, when Emmanuel and Catherine traveled to Paris to purchase furnishings for their new home. Emmanuel is holding a boll of cotton in his hand, symbolizing his success at growing cotton.

Catherine Lambre Prud'homme (1763-1848) Portrait painted in Paris, 1822.

JEAN PIERRE EMMANUEL PRUD'HOMME
(1762-1845)

1st generation to reside at Oakland Plantation

Emmanuel and his wife, Catherine initially lived in a small home on the banks of the Red River, later known as "Cane River Lake." Emmanuel grew crops of tobacco and indigo and sold the indigo to France to use as dye for French soldiers' uniforms. In 1797, he planted cotton, reputed to be the first crop of cotton to be grown on a large scale in the Louisiana Purchase territory or west of the Mississippi River.

Emancipation of Marie[3]

Emmanuel's cotton venture was a great success and other planters in the area began growing cotton. All became quite wealthy. Eli Whitney's invention of his cotton gin of 1793 increased the cultivation of cotton. The area from Natchitoches to Cloutierville in Louisiana along the Red River became known as *La Cote Joyeuse,* "the joyous coast." Oakland Plantation was also the home to many slaves whose hard work contributed significantly to the plantation's success. As farming expanded the number of these workers on the plantation increased as well.

---

[3] *Natchitoches Courier.* Published by the Milton Slocum & Co., Natchitoches, La., Monday, January 2, 1826, Limited Edition Reprints. *Courtesy Natchitoches Historic Foundation, Inc.*

In the early 1800s many of the *inhabitants* had developed close relationships with the native Indians. Emmanuel had an undiagnosed ailment that caused him considerable pain. It was perhaps arthritis. The Natchitoches' Indians who were friendly with Emmanuel told him of a place of "healing waters" and offered to take him there. In 1807 Emmanuel accepted their offer and with a servant and the necessary provisions headed for the "healing waters" or springs now known as Hot Springs, Arkansas. Emmanuel was one of the first white men to ever visit these "healing waters." Emmanuel even built a modest home there and visited frequently for a few years.[4]

In February of 1811 an Act of Congress enabled the Territory of Orleans to form a constitution and state government. Emmanuel Prud'homme and Pierre Bossier represented Natchitoches at the Constitutional Convention in New Orleans. Emmanuel and Pierre played a vital role in the framing of the Louisiana Constitution of 1812 although the Constitution primarily adopted the language of the Kentucky Constitution. After Congress approved the Constitution, the State of Louisiana was admitted into the Union.

Upon Emmanuel's return to his plantation he found his home in need of repair. Rather than repair his home he chose to build a larger home set back from the banks of the Red River. This new home was referred to as the Big House at Bermuda Plantation, also known as Prud'homme Plantation and later known as Oakland Plantation.

---

[4] Brown, Dee. *The American Spa: Hot Springs, Arkansas.* Rose Publishing Co. Little Rock, 1982

Architecture and Construction

Construction of the Big House began in 1818 and was completed in 1821. The architectural style was uniquely indigenous to Louisiana as evidenced by the materials used in its construction. The raised cottage was made of hand-hewn, heavy-pegged cypress and the walls were made of bousillage, a mixture of clay, deer hair and Spanish moss. Originally the cottage was completely surrounded by galleries (porches) supported by piers of hand-made brick. The bricks were made by hand on the plantation and sun dried. Doors opening onto the gallery had transoms. The plantation's blacksmith made the door hinges and other hardware. At times the floor-to-ceiling windows were used as passageways.

The second story was the primary living area. Originally the second story of the home had only four large rooms consisting of a parlor, dining room and two bedrooms. A chimney was placed between each pair of rooms.

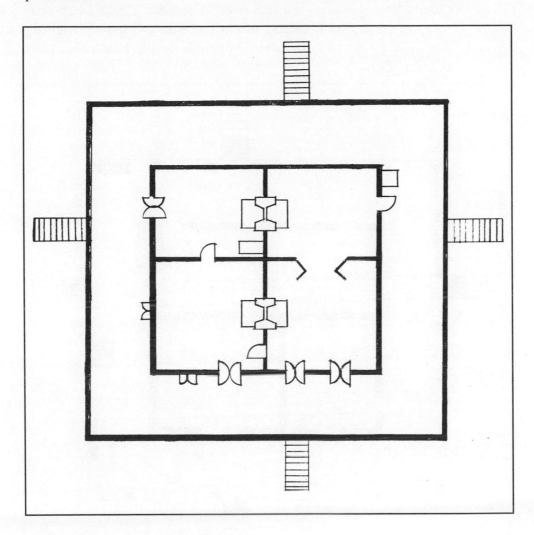

Sketch of original floor plan, second story
Courtesy Scott Payne, Student of Architecture, Louisiana State University

The first floor consisted of the mammy's room, wine cellar and storage. The mammy's room was located beneath the master bedroom. A trap door connecting the two proved beneficial when assistance with younger children was required. Access to the wine cellar on the ground floor was also via a trap door. There was a fireplace in every room of the second floor and also in the mammy's room. Originally the kitchen was in a separate building from the Big House because of the fear of fire.

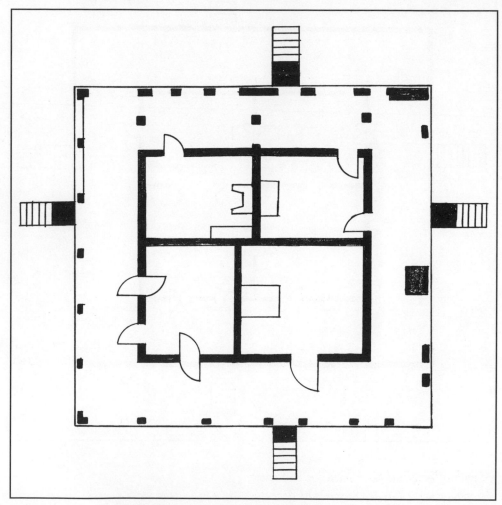

Sketch of original floor plan, ground floor
Courtesy Scott Payne, Student of Architecture, Louisiana State University

In 1880 the kitchen was brought closer to the house but remained a separate structure. The kitchen was incorporated into the main house in 1948 by enclosing a section of the west gallery. Currently the front gallery is 80 feet long and 10 feet wide. The gallery still has the original cypress flooring. Most glass panes in the windows and French doors are original glass from Switzerland. The Prud'homme Coat of Arms graces the punka in the dining room.

View of rear entry to home after kitchen incorporated to main house

When the plantation home was completed Emmanuel and Catherine Lambre Prud'homme made a journey to France for a visit. They had their portraits painted and bought furnishings for the new home. These furnishings were shipped to New Orleans in 1822 on the ship *La Jerome*. In New Orleans the furniture was placed on a barge and sent up the Mississippi River to the Red River to the plantation. Some of the original furniture remains in the home today.

Original tester bed from France (1822). Note the trundle bed underneath was used quite often by the younger Prud'homme children.

Armoire predates Oakland Plantation, it came from France with the original Prud'hommes to the New Territory in the early 1700s. Over the generations the armoire was placed on cypress blocks to accommodate the Prud'homme gentlemen as they got taller.

The Mallard Bed was purchased later by the family in New Orleans circa 1835. It is 6 feet wide, 7 feet long and 11 feet high. Shown by bed, Jane, Sandra, Kathy and Lucile Prud'homme. Courtesy Guillet Photography

The hinges are set behind the post of this armoire so that the posts swing when the doors are opened. The rocking chair was purchased later.

As early as 1822 the Prud'homme family began making changes to the home with the addition of three rooms. The rooms across the back were enlarged and a chimney was added. Over time many alterations and additions occurred. A portion of the North gallery was enclosed for a "stranger's room" which was used quite often.

During the early 1800s public accommodations for overnight stay were few and far between. The "stranger's room," while attached to the Big House, did not provide ingress to the home. It was a single room with a separate entrance providing a place for travelers to stay overnight. The use of a "strangers room" became a custom throughout the South because the visitors would bring outside news to the plantation. Reference is made to the "stranger's" room in Lestan Prud'homme's diary of June 6th, 1852 where he wrote:

...Before night I had paid a visit at Phanor's where I found my sister Julia and Mrs. Jean Janin. Jean and his lady spent the night home. Two foot-travellers (sic) were given lodgings.[5]

Side view of Oakland after the "stranger's room" and kitchen were added to the home.

[5] Lestan Prudhomme diary, 1850-1852, Irma Sompayrac Willard Collection, Cammie Henry Research Center, Northwestern State University, Natchitoches, La. (original in Howard-Tilton Memorial Library, Tulane University, New Orleans). *Courtesy Dan Willard.*

The alley of live oaks was planted in 1826. The formal gardens at Oakland Plantation were laid out in 1835. The flowerbeds were originally outlined with English Boxwoods. A few years later the old bottles were put around the beds. These bottles contained a myriad of liquors, wines and olive oils. There are bottles from Glasgow, Scotland, round bottom beer bottles from Dublin and Belfast, painted bottles from England, square bitter bottles and primarily French wine bottles.

Prud'hommes in the garden about 1958: Vivian, Lucile and Jane with her children: Kathy, Sandra and Alphonse IV.
Courtesy Guillet Photography

In 1832, Captain Henry Miller Shreve began clearing Red River of the tremendous logjam, known as the Great Raft, with a snagboat called *Archimedes*. The Great Raft essentially blocked riverboat traffic north of Natchitoches for approximately 160 miles. Captain Shreve eventually conquered the Great Raft. About this same time the Red River had cut a new channel approximately 5 miles east of Natchitoches. While both of these events served to reduce river traffic from the heart of the old settlement the planters along *La Cote Joyeuse* prospered.

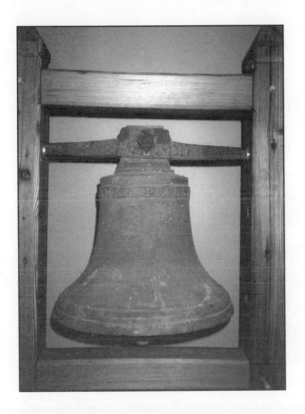

Bell and bell tower at Oakland

During the course of their marriage, Emmanuel and Catherine had eight children, two of whom died as infants. One of their twin daughters, who married at the age of 14 years, Marie Adele, died giving birth to her first child the day after Christmas 1815. One of his surviving daughters, Marie Adeline, returned to France.

Marie Adeline Prud'homme Roques (1800-1878)
Courtesy Henley Hunter

Emmanuel's oldest son, Jean Baptiste, had his own plantation and substantial commercial property in Natchitoches. In 1834 Jean Baptiste sold to his two sons, Jean Emmanuel and Gabriel St. Anne Prud'homme, his property on the corner of Horn and Front Street. Gabriel St. Anne designed iron lacework on the galleries and procured two spiral staircases, one of which still remains on the property at Horn and Front Street.

Spiral staircase, Prud'homme Building, Natchitoches

Upon Emmanuel's death he passed the Big House and substantial acreage to his son, Pierre Phanor Prud'homme, while his other children inherited other property. At that point in time the French tradition of "primogeniture" was followed and Oakland Plantation was passed on to the oldest living son of each generation.

Beau Fort Plantation

Around 1834 Emmanuel gave his son, Louis Narcisse, the plantation home now known as Beau Fort. It was built on the site of an old fort, Fort Charles. Louis Narcisse Prud'homme (1788-1844), and his wife, Marie Therese Elizabeth Metoyer (1790-1858) raised their family at Beau Fort.

Madame Louis Narcisse Prud'homme (1790-1858) (nee Marie Therese
Elizabeth Metoyer, daughter of Claude Thomas Pierre Metoyer and Marie
Therese Buard) and granddaughter, Leontine Sompayrac.
Courtesy Marty Hughes Bailey

The next owners of Beau Fort were Louis Narcisse Prud'homme II
(1807-1882) and his wife Marie Caroline Noyrit (1819-1908.) C.
Vernon Cloutier and Elizabeth Williams Cloutier restored the home
in the early to middle 1900s. Jack and Ann Williams Brittain currently own Beau Fort.

Louis Narcisse Prud'homme II (1807-1882) and wife, Marie Caroline Noyrit (1819-1908) Courtesy Cammie Henry Research Center, Northwestern State University, Natchitoches. La.

C. Vernon Cloutier (1899-1962) as a lad, owner of Beau Fort during the early and mid-1900s.

Cherokee Plantation

Legend reveals that Narcisse Prud'homme, son of Jean Pierre Emmanuel Prud'homme, built or bought Cherokee Plantation for his daughter and son-in-law, Clairesse and Emile Sompayrac. There is evidence to believe the home was built between 1800 and 1820. In 1839, Emile Sompayrac purchased the plantation from Narcisse Prud'homme. That same year, Emile Sompayrac's plantation was the site of the Gaiennie-Bossier duel.

A heated political argument between General Francois Gaiennie of Cloutierville, a Whig, and General Pierre Bossier, a Democrat resulted in the infamous duel of 1839. Phanor Prud'homme I of Oakland Plantation, Emile Sompayrac and other Creoles witnessed the duel. As legend goes, Gaiennie's first shot intentionally missed Bossier as he did not want to kill his friend. Bossier's aim was dead on. For the rest of his life, Pierre Bossier regretted killing his friend. The Parish of Bossier was named after Pierre Bossier.

In 1891 the property was sold to Robert Calvert Murphy. His granddaughter and her husband, Mr. and Mrs. William Nolan, currently own it.

Pierre Jean Baptiste Evariste Bossier (1794-1844) son of Francois Paul Bossier and Catherine Pelage Lambre. Courtesy Marty Hughes Bailey

Oaklawn Plantation

Oaklawn Plantation was built by, or for, Achille Prud'homme, son of L. Narcisse Prud'homme and Elizabeth Metoyer, around 1835. Achille married Mary Estelle Prud'homme Feb 16, 1848 and they had several children. Achille died March 14, 1864 just before General Banks and his Union troops were retreating from the Battle of Mansfield. There are two legends as to how Oaklawn was spared the ravages of the Union army during the Red River Campaign. One story is that the widow Estelle Prud'homme had her children wear red caps, in support of the Union as the troops passed in front of her home. Another story is that the widow Estelle dressed one of her daughters in a scarlet red cloak, an indication of scarlet fever, and sat her on the gallery as the Union troops passed.

After the war Oaklawn was lost to carpetbaggers. In 1903 the home was bought back into the Prud'homme family. It was purchased by Adeline Prud'homme Cloutier and her husband, Charles Edgar Cloutier. Bobby Harling, author of *Steel Magnolias*, currently owns Oaklawn.

Charles Edgar Cloutier,
(1867-1935) husband of
Adeline Prud'homme
Cloutier (1875-1968)
Courtesy Conna Cloutier

Charles Vernon (1899-1962)
and Pierre Emmanuel Cloutier,
(1901-1977)
children of Edgar and Adeline

Pierre Phanor Prud'homme
(1807-1865)

2nd generation to reside at Oakland Plantation

Pierre Phanor (hereinafter referred to as "Phanor") returned to the family plantation following his education in France and continued the family tradition as a planter. As was the case in much of the South during this era, the agricultural success of many plantations depended on the use of slaves and Oakland Plantation was no different. Agriculture expanded immensely during this period of time. Phanor managed the plantation with the help of his overseer while the workers tilled the soil.

Pierre Phanor
Prud'homme
(1807-1865)

A daily account of Phanor Prud'homme's farming operations can be found in his farm journal.[6]   Phanor's cotton book of 1836 appears to have been written by Phanor's overseer, J. F. Culbertson. It reveals cottonpicking for the season began on Monday, August 29, 1836. During the harvest season cotton was picked seven days a week. Some of the workers contributing to the success at Oakland during 1836 were: Dorceno, Jupiter, Zeek, Charles, Lewis, Phil, Alexee, Alexan, Grigwa, Albert, Azeas, Azeastan, Lolestan, Tebo, Tousant, Jesse, Nora, Machel, Bob, Afred, Augustus, George, Solomon, Paul, Jim, Martan, Philip, Johnston, Paschal, Antoine, Breno, Jack, Butten, Lucky, Malinzo, B Liza, Martha, Rachel, Mino, Zano, Betsy, Anyco, Tempy, Nancy, Harriet, Tonet, Teres, Angelio, Barbo, Rose, Judic, Tom, Suset, Sally, Tisant, Lizy, Roset, Elan, Dofy, Frank, Eli, Nathan, L. J. Love, Danzelle, Celeste, Artemize, Lardan, Marie, Polly, Claresse, Barry, Lily, Archeal, Ellen, Moses, Ramo and Louise. [7]

---

[6] The Prudhomme Family Papers, Collection #613 (folder 267), Southern Historical Collection, Wilson Library, University of North Carolina at Chapel Hill.

[7] Ibid

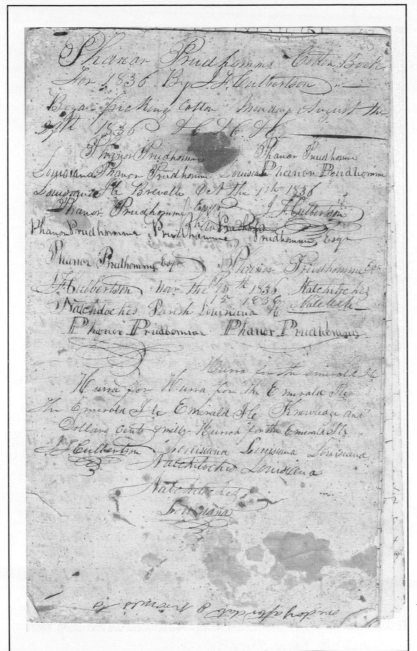

Phanor Prud'homme's Cotton Book[8]

8 Ibid

In 1835 Phanor married Susanne "Lise" Metoyer, daughter of Francois Benjamin Metoyer (b.1794) and M. Aurore Lambre. Lise's grandparents were Claude Thomas Pierre Metoyer and Marie Therese Buard. Phanor and Lise raised five children at Oakland. Many accounts of their lifestyle can be found in Lestan Prud'homme's diary of 1850-1852. Lestan was Phanor's first cousin and his diary reveals a prolific Creole social lifestyle along *La Cote Joyeuse* during the 1850s.

Marie Aurore Lambre Metoyer (1798-1877), mother of Lise Metoyer Prud'homme and Cephalide Metoyer Archinard Prud'homme. Courtesy Norman and Sand Marmillion, Laura Plantation

Lestan Prud'homme (1801-1876) and Elisa Elizabeth Lambre, the diarist's parents.

Lestan Prud'homme's father's plantation was adjacent to Oakland and Lestan dined frequently at Phanor's table. He seemed quite smitten with Phanor's daughter's female companions. Phanor's oldest daughter, Adeline was a boarder at Sacred Heart Convent in Natchitoches along with her first cousin, Desiree Archinard. The girls of this generation were referred to as the Belles of *La Cote Joyeuse*. Lestan's visits to Phanor's home were more frequent when Sacred Heart Convent was closed and the Belles were home for the summer. *Soirees* were frequently enjoyed at the plantation as well as at Phanor's town home in Natchitoches.

*Lestan Prud'homme
(Diarist) Grandson of
Antoine Prud'homme
Courtesy Conna Cloutier*

While socializing with the extended family was frequent, Phanor's home also provided a private school for his younger children and relatives. Education was emphasized and the family library was extensive. The library included the works of Voltaire, Buffon, Rousseau, Moliere, Merilhou, LaHarpe, Diderot and Boileau. Most of the books were written in French.

Phanor supervised the planting and his wife, Lise, tended to the children. Unfortunately tragedy struck the home when Lise became ill. Lestan Prud'homme's diary reveals an emotional account of the grief the family experienced during the illness and death of Phanor's wife. His diary of May 12, 1852 reveals the first sign of Lise's illness: "Mrs. Phanor fell sick this morning with the fever and is suffering much with a pain in her shoulder." Lestan provides an almost daily account of her disease progression. On May 17, 1852 two physicians opined Lise had only one chance in nine hundred ninety-nine of surviving.

On May 19, 1852, Lestan wrote:

The house was full with the relations of the deceased, all crying and plunged in the deepest sorrow, nothing but sorrow, sobbing and mourning. Never shall I forget the appearance and attitude of the deceased unfortunate husband; his face bathed in tears, his eyes almost wild with the feelings that tore his bosom, when coming up to several gentlemen and I who were in the gallery. He addressed us in the following words; 'It is all over, my poor Lise is no more!' Then strongly grasping his breast with a convulsive motion he remained a few words silent, and as resuming the command of his mind, he continued, 'tis now I need courage, where are my poor children.' From this he darted forward like an arrow and flew to the embrace of his children, who were crying and shrieking at the loss of their dear mother...[9]

Suzanne Lise Metoyer Prud'homme (1818-1852) Phanor's first wife

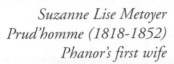

---

[9] Lestan Prudhomme diary, 1850-1852, Irma Sompayrac Willard Collection, Cammie Henry Research Center, Northwestern State University, Natchitoches, La. (original in Howard–Tilton Memorial Library, Tulane University, New Orleans). *Courtesy Dan Willard.*

At the time of her death, Lise's oldest child, Adeline was eighteen, Alphonse was fourteen, Emma was twelve, Pierre Emmanuel was eight and her youngest, Henriette, four. During this tragic point in time, Lise's sister, Cephalide Metoyer Archinard, a widow who lived at a neighboring plantation, helped immensely with the caring and raising of the children. Three years later, Phanor married Cephalide. The marriage was welcomed as Cephalide had always been close to her sister's children. Phanor too, raised Cephalide's children, Desiree and Irene, as his own. Unfortunately, death was no stranger to the family. The only child born to Cephalide and Phanor died as an infant. In addition, Phanor's daughter, Emma, died in 1854 and Cephalide died in 1857.

Cephalide Metoyer Archinard Prud'homme
(1817-1857) Phanor's second wife
(sister to his first wife, Lise)
Courtesy Norman and Sand Marmillion
of Laura Plantation

In 1860 Phanor owned approximately 3,400 acres although much of this land was undeveloped and not suitable for farming. Raising livestock was also a vital part of the plantation. Many of the workers were allowed to own and raise livestock on the plantation.[10] Cotton remained the primary crop while food crops also continued to be grown. A *Daily Record of Passing Events on Phanor Prud'homme's Plantation* was kept in 1860 by his overseer, Seneca Pace.[11] This daily record includes notations about the weather and the crops, as well as more personal entries. For instance, the entry for Tuesday, January 17, 1860 reveals the hands having time off to attend the funeral of a fellow hand, Tousant. Construction of the Overseer's house began in 1861.

During this time Phanor's youngest daughter, Henriette, was at a boarding school in New Orleans. His oldest daughter, Adeline, married Winter Wood Breazeale in 1856 and they resided on the Breazeale plantation about 20 miles south of Natchitoches with their eleven children: Hopkins Payne, Phanor, Upshur, Winter Wood, Marie Lise, Maude Manette, Mabel Josephine (twin), Joseph Malcolm (twin), Marie Manette, Drury Wood, and Ross Edmund.

W. W. Breazeale (1827-1896), husband of Catherine Adeline Prud'homme (1836-1878) Courtesy Conna Cloutier

---

10 The Prudhomme Family Papers, Collection, Southern Historical Collection, Wilson Library, University of North Carolina at Chapel Hill.

11 The Prudhomme Family Papers, Collection, Southern Historical Collection, Wilson Library, University of North Carolina at Chapel Hill.

*Phanor Breazeale (1858-1934)
son of Catherine Adeline
Prud'homme and Col. Winter
Wood Breazeale. Phanor Breazeale
served 3 terms in the United States
Congress, 1899-1905.*

*Desiree Buard Breazeale (1870-1969) and Winter Wood Breazeale II
(1863-1940) son of Catherine Adeline Prud'homme. Desiree was
reared at the Duparc-Locoul Plantation (Laura Plantation)
Courtesy Mary Breazeale Cunningham*

Phanor's oldest son, Jacques Alphonse I, was preparing to attend college at Yale at New Haven, Connecticut, but before entering his father called him home due to the intense sectional feeling over the Kansas-Nebraska Bill. Instead Alphonse I attended the University of Virginia from 1856 to 1858 and then transferred to the University of North Carolina. Phanor's son, Pierre Emmanuel II, entered Georgetown University at the age of 15 years.

Phanor's stepdaughter (and niece) Desiree, married Emile Locoul and moved to her husband's plantation in south Louisiana later known as Laura Plantation. Coincidentally this was the same plantation where Phanor's Aunt Nanette Prud'homme DuParc lived. Desiree returned to Oakland in 1861 with her infant daughter, Laura, in an attempt to escape the ravages of the Civil War, but her plan was foiled, as *La Cote Joyeuse* did not escape the war.

Desiree Archinard Locoul
and daughter, Laura
Courtesy Norman and Sand
Marmillion of Laura Plantation

The Civil War

When the "war between the states" started in 1861, Jacques Alphonse was working as an engineer following his graduation from the University of North Carolina. Pierre Emmanuel had recently returned home from Georgetown University because of the rebellion. Both sons joined the Confederate army. Alphonse enlisted in Company G, 3rd Louisiana Infantry. He was acting orderly sergeant of his company at the battle of Elkhorn Tavern March 7, 1862, when he was wounded and captured.[12] Ten days later he escaped and rejoined his company. He was discharged briefly for his wounds but soon reentered the services. He and Col. Winter Wood Breazeale organized a cavalry battalion of five companies. He was again severely injured at the battle of Irish Bend April 14, 1864 but continued to serve.

Jacques Alphonse Prud'homme (1838-1919)

---

12 The battle of Elkhorn Tavern was known also as the battle of Pea Ridge. The Pea Ridge Campaign by Sigel, Major-General Franz, U. S. V. The Battles and Leaders of the Civil War, Castle, Secaucus, N.J.

During the war Alphonse frequently wrote to his father. At a camp near Springfield, Missouri, on Wednesday, August 14th 1861, Alphonse wrote to his father about the death of his dear friend and cousin Placide Bossier:

Dear Father,

At the time of writing my last, July 30th, we were under marching orders.…Often I have heard of battle, now I can say I've seen one.…Was it not the loss of my esteemed friend Placide, it would be a battle that I would never have regretted. Never, however, can I think of that day without a shadow of regret. A truer and more constant friend than he never lived; I loved him as a brother; our ranks could not afford a better soldier —ever ready for duty—never murmuring at the numerous trials which fell to our lot—brave as himself, he rushed in the thickest fire, and acted his part cooly (sic) and deliberately, when he received the fatal wound, none were in advance of him, knowing that he could not live, he attempted to speak, but could only whisper 'I'm suffocating'! He appeared cool and quiet, and undoubtedly met death like a man and a Christian. I could not stay to see him die, I bade him good-bye, pressed his hand and promised to avenge him. I saw from his eyes that he understood me. He beckoned to me with his hands to hand him his canteen, then bade me, go. I left him in charge of Blount, but he died shortly after, even before the Surgeon could reach him. He lived only about ten minutes. We burried (sic) him as well as possible, that his body may be recovered if desired. Not forgetting in that moment of sorrow, his dear mother and sisters upon whom his death will no doubt fill heavily. I cut a large lock of his hair which Mr. Dicharry has had the kindness to place in his trunk. I have also his prayer book, which I will put in some secure place to take back to them.

Your affectionate son,
J. Alp'h PRUDHOMME[13]

---

[13] Odalie Prud'homme Scrapbook, Carmen Breazeale Collection, Cammie Henry Research Center, Northwestern State University, Natchitoches, La

Placide Bossier was a private in the Company G, Third Regiment Pelican Rangers, Louisiana Infantry. The loss of Placide at the age of 23 years at the battle of Oak Hill, Mo. was felt by the entire community, as were the deaths of many soldiers. Placide was the son of Jules Victor Bosssier and M. Lise Victorie Desiree Sompayrac. He now lies in the Catholic Cemetery, Natchitoches, Louisiana.

Major General J. A. Prudhomme and Staff of Louisiana Division, U. C. V.

LIEUT. COL. R. T. WALSHE,   GEN. A. B. BOOTH,   GEN. J. A. PRUDHOMME,   COL. T. W. CASPLEMAN,   GEN. LEON JASTREMSKI,   GEN. W. H. TUNNARD,   MAJ. D. S. SULLIVAN,
   Commissionary General.   Past Major General.   Major Gen'l Commanding.   Adj. Gen. and Ch of Staff.   Past Major General.   Past Major General.   Aid-de-camp.
LIEUT. COL. L. B. CLAIBORNE,   MAJ. S. R. HARMANSON,   MAJOR I. CASPARI.   MAJOR J. P. HIGGINS,   MAJOR J. W. GAINS,   MAJOR F. D. TUNNARD,   MAJOR L. M. COSTLEY,
   Judge Advocate General.   Aide-de-camp.   Aide-de-camp.   Aide-de-camp.   Asst. Quartermaster General. Aide-de-camp.   Aide-de-camp.
      MAJOR R. S. PROSSER,   LIEUT. COL. ALDEN McLELLAN,   MAJOR W. W. LEAKE,   MAJOR O. D. BROOKS,
   Assistant Chaplain General.   Quartermaster General.   Aide-de-camp.   Assistant Commissary General.
               SHREVEPORT, LA., OCTOBER 9, 1907.

Courtesy Noel Memorial Library,
LSU-Shreveport Archives

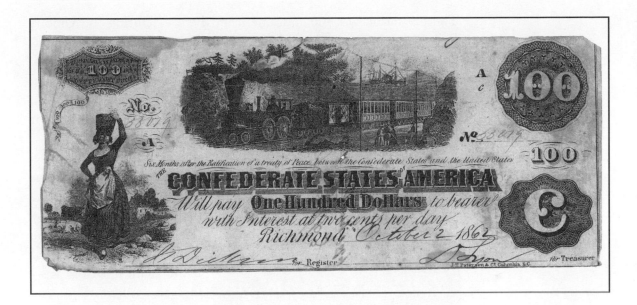

Confederate bond

Phanor's younger son, Pierre Emmanuel, became a member of the Prud'homme Guards. He was taken prisoner with the surrender of Vicksburg but was soon paroled. He was later promoted to Orderly Sergeant and remained as such until the end of the war.

Phanor, who was elderly, remained at the plantation with his family as well as other extended family members who sought refuge at the plantation during the war. During the Civil War cotton farming continued. Food crops were grown to sustain those living on the plantation.

The plantation was not immune from the war. During the Union's Red River Campaign of 1864, General Nathaniel Banks and his troops paid an unannounced visit to Bermuda (Oakland) Plantation. At that time these troops were burning and looting the countryside. They burned Jacques Alphonse's fiance's home, Magnolia Plantation, and would have burned the Big House at Oakland had it not been for the pleas of the faithful workers.

Phanor was quite paternalistic with the workers and the loyalty was mutual. While the Big House was spared, General Banks burned the cotton gin. Over 1000 bales of Prud'homme cotton were burned by

Confederates to keep the cotton out of General Banks' hands. Before leaving the plantation one member of the Yankee troops drove his saber through the portrait of Lise Metoyer Prud'homme, Phanor's deceased first wife. The troops left the Big House structure intact but took Pierre Phanor as prisoner and made him march with them to Natchitoches.

Lise Metoyer Prud'homme. Note the hole in portrait made from a Union soldier's saber during Red River Campaign of 1864.

52

While marching to Natchitoches, Phanor, who was elderly and in poor health, collapsed along the wayside and the troops left him. Phanor was later found by family members and taken to the town home of Ambrose LeComte in Natchitoches. Relatives cared for Phanor in Natchitoches but he died before ever being able to return to his plantation.

Although the casualties of the war were great they did not stop Jacques Alphonse from marrying his betrothed, Elisa LeComte, of Magnolia Plantation in 1864. Alphonse and Elisa's wedding cake was embellished with a miniature silken Confederate flag. Throughout the war Elisa frequently wrote letters to Alphonse expressing her concerns and prayers for his safe return.

Ambrose LeComte II (1807-1883) of Magnolia Plantation, father of Elisa LeComte Prud'homme

Magnolia Plantation (rebuilt in 1889) Home of Elisa LeComte prior to her marriage to J. Alphonse Prud'homme. Yankees burned the original home.

Jacques Alphonse Prud'homme
(1838-1919)

3rd generation to reside at Oakland Plantation

THE RECONSTRUCTION

The Civil War brought an end to the antebellum lifestyle of *La Cote Joyeuse*. After the war, the two sons, Jacques Alphonse and Pierre Emmanuel returned to rehabilitate the devastated plantation. They continued farming in spite of the post war obstacles facing them. Cotton was planted. While many of the workers left the plantation after the war, many remained on Oakland. Two of the many families remaining at Oakland to work for contract labor were those of Solomon Wilson, the carpenter and Solomon Williams, the blacksmith.

Initially, Alphonse and Pierre Emmanuel and their families lived on the plantation along with the workers that chose to remain. Alphonse and his wife, Elisa, had eight children: Pierre Phanor, Jules Lecomte, Edward Carrington, Marie Cora, Marie Atala, Julia Eleanore, Marie Maie and Marie Noelie

Jacques Alphonse Prud'homme (1838-1919) and his wife, Elisa LeComte Prud'homme (1840-1923)

Jacques Alphonse with daughters, Cora (7 years) and Atala "Lallah" (3 years)
Courtesy Mildred "Mimi" Methvin

Julia and Noelie Prud'homme, 1903, (Note bell tower in background) Courtesy Cammie Henry Research Center, Northwestern State University, Natchitoches. La. Henley Hunter Collection

Phanor's daughter, Henriette, married Dr. Blount Baker Breazeale in 1865 and lived in the Natchitoches town home. Their children were James Wilmer, Elisha Winter, Evariste Overton Walter, Jack Alphonse and Marie Emma. Times were extremely difficult during the carpet-bag government. Many a time Henrietta wrote to her brothers requesting whether they had vegetables from the plantation to share. The Reconstruction period was difficult to say the least but the family persevered.

Henriette Prud'homme Breazeale (1842-1922) and family members: Front row: Emma and Mary Keator Breazeale. Second row: Wilmer, Henriette and Elisha Winter Breazeale. Back row: Laiza Lambre Breazeale. Courtesy Conna Cloutier

As the financial situation improved, the plantation was divided between the two brothers. The older son, Alphonse, took the Big House and land west of the Red River. Pierre Emmanuel and his wife, Julia Buard, took the land east of the Red River. Bermuda Plantation had essentially been divided. Alphonse gave his plantation the name of "Oakland Plantation" because the live oaks planted in 1826 had grown significantly forming an alley from the river to the home. Pierre Emmanuel named his plantation "Ataho" for the Ataho River that ran through his property.

Pierre Emmanuel Prud'homme (1844-1934) and his wife, Julia Buard

Ataho Plantation – Pierre Emmanuel Prud'homme (1844-1934)

Pierre Emmanuel continued his cotton farming at Ataho Plantation. Ataho and Oakland are listed on the National Register of Historic Places under the name of the "Jean Pierre Emmanuel Prud'homme Plantation."

Pierre Emmanuel and his family lived in the home after Bermuda Plantation was divided following the Civil War. Pierre Emmanuel's children were Ovide, Felix, Laura, Suzanne Lise "Te Tee", Charles Edwin (died at age 11 years) Cecile, Raymond Frances Emile and Adeline.

Ataho Plantation. Currently, Marti Vienne, a descendant of the Prud'hommes, and her family, live at Ataho as her ancestors have since the Reconstruction period

Unfortunately the original home burned in 1873. The home was rebuilt circa 1877 with materials from the Big House at Oakland. A wing (*garconniere*) of the Big House was removed and transferred to Pierre Emmanuel's land to rebuild his home.

The garconniere was the quarters used by the male Creole family members. Lestan Prud'homme refers to the garconniere in his diary on Holy Saturday, March 30th, 1850:

There was service in the church this morning; there was none in the evening. My Aunt Benjamin, Leonce, my Uncle Cloutier and his son John came in town. We were seven in a very small room at Phanor's called <u>la garconniere,</u> and as all did not come in together, we did not get to sleep before midnight, and as out of three beds we had to make room for seven none slept too much. I went to confession to go to communion tomorrow.[14]

[14] Lestan Prudhomme diary, 1850-1852, Irma Sompayrac Willard Collection, Cammie Henry Research Center, Northwestern State University, Natchitoches, La (original in Howard–Tilton Memorial Library, Tulane University, New Orleans). *Courtesy Dan Willard.*

Family in front of Ataho, 1903 **Front row:** *Reginald Prud'homme (child), Pierre Emanuel Prud'homme, Charles Edward "Bennie" Dranguet (child), Julie Buard Prud'homme* **Back row:** *Unknown, Felix Prud'homme, Laura Prud'homme, Suzanne Lise "Te Tee" Prud'homme Dranguet, Julie Dranguet (child), Cele Prud'homme, Adeline Prud'homme Cloutier. Courtesy Marti Williamson Vienne*

In 1877 tragedy again struck the families when their cousin, Jules Lambre, drowned in Cane River attempting to save a young boy. Jules left his widow, Odalie Prud'homme Lambre, with six small children to raise alone.

Widow Odalie Prud'homme Lambre, daughter of J.J. Lestan Prud'homme and Marie Eleysa Lambre, with her children, Angela, Octave, Valsin, Ursin, Lafon, and Laiza. Courtesy Conna Cloutier

Odalie Prud'homme Lambre's home. Courtesy Mr. and Mrs. Ross Gwinn

Jules Lambre, son of Valsin Lambre and Clarissa Hertzog. On the back of the photo Odalie wrote the following inscription:

Jules Lambre 1877
Dear Children,

    This likeness was recopied (after your poor father's death) from a likeness which he had given to Mama in 1866 shortly before his marriage.

    It is the most precious souvenir we have from him. I treasure it above all things, you must do the same and never part from it. Whenever you have any flowers place a bouquet in your mother's name and never forget to pray for your beloved Papa who adored all of you and your broken hearted mother who lived but for him.
The joy of living is gone forever. [15]

---

[15] *Courtesy Conna Cloutier*

The Blacksmith, Solomon Williams

The talented blacksmith, Solomon Williams, was an invaluable member of Oakland Plantation. Many of Solomon's works are still evident on the plantation today. While Solomon was born into slavery and freed after the Civil War, he remained at the plantation. He was reputed to have been very strong, over six feet tall with a long white beard in his later years. Solomon's wife was Laide Williams. Solomon made many contributions to farming. In addition, he made door latches and hardware for the home, as well as iron grave markers and wrought iron drilling equipment.

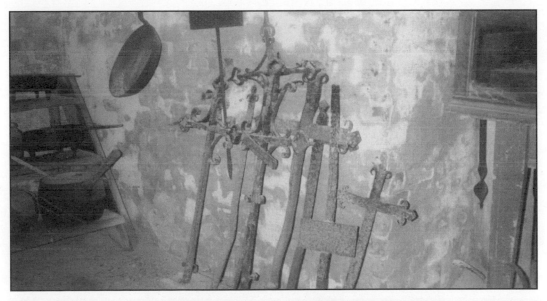

Crosses from slave cemetery made by Solomon, the blacksmith. One of these crosses bears the name of Solomon's wife: "LAIDE WILLIAMS DIED JAN 21/87 AGE 47"

According to tradition, the well drilling tools were designed by a French engineer and made by Solomon Williams. The purpose of the equipment was drilling for water. The family had been plagued by bouts of cholera and other ailments thought to be caused from the impure river water. The initial drilling expeditions produced mere "swamp gas" but later water was found. After water was hit and the tools no longer needed, they were buried on the plantation and forgotten for about 100 years. They were accidentally found on the plantation in 1924. These drilling tools are believed to be some of the oldest drilling tools in existence.

Well drilling tools made by Solomon Williams circa 1823.

After the Civil War Solomon Williams remained at Oakland Plantation but he negotiated contracts independently for his labor because of his special skills. Legend has it that his son left the plantation during the war and joined the Union Army.

Blacksmith Shop

In the 1980s a lady from California who was a descendant of the Williams family visited Oakland in search of information about her ancestors. Initially she thought her ancestors were from a plantation in the Bermuda Islands, not realizing there was a Bermuda, Louisiana. Nonetheless her persistence paid off as her continued searching led her to Oakland Plantation. My grandmother, Lucile Prud'homme, helped her find documentation tracing her ancestors to Oakland.

The Carpenter, Solomon Wilson (1815-1873)

Solomon Wilson was the head carpenter. He was born in Virginia in 1815. While born into slavery he was freed after the Civil War, and like Solomon Williams, negotiated contracts for his labor after the war.[16]

Carpenter Shop

[16] A detailed account of the workers remaining at Oakland Plantation can be found in the Prudhomme Family Papers, Southern Historical Collection, Wilson Library, University of North Carolina at Chapel Hill.

"Old Aunt Marie" believed to be the widow of Solomon Wilson. Marie was 105 years old at the time the photo was taken in 1934.

The Plantation Lathe

The Plantation Doctor

In 1866 Dr. Joseph Leveque and his family relocated to the Cane River community. Following the Civil War Dr. Leveque lost his plantation in South Louisiana to carpetbaggers. Jacques Alphonse Prud'homme welcomed the newcomer as the assistance of a physician to keep the workers healthy was necessary for the survival of the plantation.

Dr. Leveque was provided a cottage on the plantation where he and Mrs. Leveque raised their children, Lucie and Joseph, Jr. They lived on the plantation for many years. Dr. Leveque adapted well at Oakland

Plantation. The community admired and cherished Dr. Leveque and his feeling for the community was mutual. His daughter, Lucie, married Lambre Prud'homme but later divorced. June was the only child born to Lucie and Lambre.

Lucie Leveque Prud'homme
Courtesy Northwestern State University of Louisiana, Watson Memorial Library, Cammie G. Henry Research Center, Irma Sompayrac Willard Collection

Lambre Prud'homme
Courtesy Northwestern State University of Louisiana, Watson Memorial
Library, Cammie G. Henry Research Center, Irma Sompayrac Willard
Collection

As time passed, Mrs. Leveque grew tired of living in the cottage on the plantation and wanted a home of her own. Dr. Leveque remained on the plantation but Mrs. Leveque, Lucie, June and Joseph, Jr. moved to New York City. Lucie styled herself an actress and began a stage career. Her stage name was Roda Camerine. Joseph, Jr. pursued his acting career in London and was known as the "Hapless Harlequin."

Meanwhile, back on the plantation, Dr. Leveque continued his profession of providing care to the infirm. A chimney fire erupted at the Big House on Oakland Plantation. Dr. Leveque assisted in the bucket brigade as water was hauled from the grounds, up the stairs, across the gallery and to the slate roof. The fire was successfully extinguished, but unfortunately, the following day, Dr. Leveque was found dead at the cottage. He was 62 years old.

After Dr. Leveque's death members of the Prud'homme family moved into the cottage. Prud'homme descendants continued to occupy the cottage for years. Later the cottage was passed on to Marie Adele Prud'homme and her husband, Jesse Brett. The Brett's daughter, Doris Ann Brett Vincent, inherited the cottage and shared Dr. Leveque's story with me. Mrs. Vincent sold the cottage and acreage to the National Park Service in 1998.

Doctor's Cottage, 1957
Courtesy Doris Ann Brett Vincent

*Mayo Prud'homme, Doris Ann Brett and Vivian
Prud'homme on the gallery at Oakland.*

Doris Ann Brett with cousins, Alex and Keith Cloutier

*Jesse Emmett and Adele Prud'homme Brett
at the cottage, 1972. Courtesy Doris Ann Brett Vincent*

The Overseer

The overseer at Oakland held a position of prestige. The cotton book of 1836 shows the overseer at that point in time as J. F. Culbertson.[17] Lestan Prudhomme's diary lists Mr. Russell as the overseer in 1852.[18] It was Seneca Pace, the overseer during 1861, who oversaw the building of the overseer's house. The square raised cottage sits on brick piers with a hip roof. The walls, like that of the Big House, were constructed with wood and filled with bousillage.

Camille and Leo Metoyer at the Overseer's house.
Courtesy Leo and Mary Sue Metoyer

---

[17] The Prudhomme Family Papers, Collection #613 (folder 267), Southern Historical Collection, Wilson Library, University of North Carolina at Chapel Hill.

[18] Lestan Prudhomme diary, 1850-1852, Irma Sompayrac Willard Collection, Cammie Henry Research Center, Northwestern State University, Natchitoches, La (original in Howard–Tilton Memorial Library, Tulane University, New Orleans). *Courtesy Dan Willard.*

During and after the Civil war the position of overseer was held by a variety of men while Seneca Pace served in the Confederate army. During the early 1900's Rene Metoyer was overseer for Pierre Phanor Prud'homme. He and his wife, Suzette raised their family on Oakland Plantation. Rene Metoyer's son, Leo Louis Metoyer continued in his father's footsteps as overseer to the second Alphonse Prud'homme as well as to Alphonse III and Kenneth Prud'homme.

Suzette Metoyer
Courtesy Leo and Mary Sue Metoyer

Leo Metoyer was raised in the Overseer's house in the early 1900's. In addition, he and his wife, Camille raised their children there from 1933 through 1977. A very close relationship existed between the Metoyers and the Prud'hommes. The Metoyers are descendants of the Metoyers from Melrose Plantation in Isle Brevelle.

Children of Leo and Camille, Leo and Mary Sue
Courtesy Leo and Mary Sue Metoyer

Leo Metoyer, overseer, with cattle.
Courtesy Leo and Mary Sue Metoyer

Melrose

Daughter of Leo and Camille, Josephine, at wedding reception with husband, Larry DuBriel, 1961, in overseer's house. Courtesy Leo and Mary Sue Metoyer

Jules "Uncle Buddy" Lecomte Prud'homme

The Plantation Store

In or about 1874, Jacques Alphonse established the plantation's store that was similar to a commissary. While one of its functions was to provide supplies for the plantation, it also contributed to the social aspects of the community. Provisions reached the store via barges and riverboats coming up the river. Jacques Alphonse used one room in the store as his office. In later years the store would also serve as a post office and temporary residence for Jacques Alphonse's son, Jules "Uncle Buddy" Lecomte Prud'homme.

Oakland Plantation Store with Pigeonnier in background.
Back of photo states: " PaPas Store Feb. 1878 Bud, Albert, Lallah by Nancy (Nurse)
2 yrs. 4mos old; Phonse, Alain Metoyer Dog Queen John"

Oakland Store circa 1930s

At the turn of the century Oakland Plantation consisted of about 1200 acres. Tenant farming was implemented but short lived most probably because of the invasion of the boll weevil. The infamous boll weevil reached Louisiana about 1903. It entered this country from Mexico and spread quickly through Texas to Louisiana devastating the cotton industry for several more years.

Notwithstanding the boll weevil's destruction, in 1904 Alphonse exhibited his cotton at the Louisiana Purchase exposition at the World's Fair in St. Louis and in the Jamestown exposition in 1907. He won gold metals in each instance.

Prud'hommes with cotton bale
Courtesy Northwestern State University of Louisiana, Watson Memorial Library,
Cammie G. Henry Research Center, Henley Hunter Collection

Prud'hommes with wagon load of cotton
Courtesy Northwestern State University of Louisiana, Watson Memorial Library,
Cammie G. Henry Research Center, Henley Hunter Collection

Pierre Phanor Prud'homme II
(1865-1948)

4th generation to reside at Oakland Plantation

Pierre Phanor Prud'homme II
4 years of age (1869)

Pierre Phanor II was reared at Oakland Plantation with his siblings. All the children received a Catholic education.

Education

Pierre Phanor II was educated at the University of Notre Dame from 1883 to 1888. During that point in time Notre Dame enrolled students of grade school and high school age, referred to as *Minims.* Phanor II enrolled as a *Minim* and graduated from the college with a Certificate of Telegraphy in 1885 and a Commercial Diploma in 1888. His brothers, Jules and Edward, also attended the University of Notre Dame as *Minims.*

Edward Carrington Prud'homme (1869-1941) began Notre Dame in 1883 at the age of 14 years and graduated in1891. He participated on the rowing team. He was also a member of the first football team and captain of the football team for the 1888-1889 season.

Interestingly, in 1953 another descendant of Emmanuel Prud'homme, Michael Edwin "Ed" Prud'homme, was also a member of the Notre Dame football team. Ed Prud'homme's father was Lynn Xavier Prud'homme, son of Ellen "Nellie" Eck and Jean (John) Baptiste Prud'homme. Jean (John) Baptiste (1859-1913) was the son of Louis Gabriel Prud'homme (1831-1899) and Marie Emerante Lambre (1837-1916) of Rosa Plantation in Campti, Louisiana. After the Civil War Jean (John) Baptiste settled in Texarkana. Louis Gabriel was the son of Gabriel Ailhaud St. Anne Prud'homme (1808-1865) and Marie Aglae Prud'homme (1813-1901), daughter of Louis Narcisse Prud'homme, I (1788-1844) and Marie Therese Elisabeth Metoyer (1790-1858) of Beau Fort Plantation. Gabriel St. Anne Prud'homme was the son of Jean Baptiste Prud'homme, II (1785-1861) and Marie Therese Victoire Ailhaud St. Anne. Jean Baptiste II and Louis Narcisse I were sons of Emmanuel Prud'homme of Oakland Plantation.

The University of Notre Dame's first football team, 1887.
Front row: H. Jewett, J. Cusack, H. Luhn, E. Prud'homme
Back row: J. Hepburn, G. Houck, E. Sawkins, F. Fehr, P. Nelson, E. Melady, F. Springer.
Courtesy The University of Notre Dame Archives and Kathleen Prud'homme Batten

Most of Phanor's sisters were educated by The Daughters of the Cross while boarding at St. Vincent's Academy in Shreveport, Louisiana. One sister attended St. Mary's Academy in Natchitoches.

St. Vincent's Academy graduating class of 1895: Maie Prud'homme front right, Julia Prud'homme, back right. Others in photo: Genie Burt, Ethel Dillon, Anna Price, Nina Chopin and Annie March. Courtesy LSU-Shreveport Archives, Coll. 354 St. Vincent's Academy

Atala "Lallah" Prud'homme (1875-1958)

Upon Pierre Phanor's graduation from the University of Notre Dame, he returned to Oakland Plantation to continue farming and running the store. Pierre Phanor took over operations of the plantation in 1919 following the death of his father.

Phanor's Family

Nine children were born to Pierre Phanor and his wife Marie Laure Cloutier: James Alphonse, Louise Vivian, Elisa Elizabeth, Marie Adele, Marie Leanore (infant), Pierre Phanor (infant), Pierre Phanor, Marie Lucie, Louis Donald. Two children died as infants and the daughter, Louise Vivian, died at the age of six years.

Pierre Phanor Prud'homme (1865-1948) and wife, Marie Laure Cloutier (1871-1941)

James Alphonse
Prud'homme II
(1896-1991)

Alphonse II, Vivian, who died shortly
after photo was taken in 1905, and Lisa.

Alphonse II and Lisa (circa 1915)
Courtesy Mr. and Mrs. Arnold Cloutier

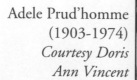

Adele Prud'homme
(1903-1974)
Courtesy Doris
Ann Vincent

James Alphonse Prud'homme II
(1896-1991)

5th and 6th generations to live at Oakland

James Alphonse II was better known as "Phonsie" to his contemporaries and as "PawPaw" to his grandchildren. Alphonse was raised on the plantation with his siblings. In 1919 Alphonse II was stationed in Paris, France following World War I. His grandfather, Jacques Alphonse, died while Alphonse II was in Paris.

Lucile Keator was born in Webster Groves, Missouri, but she had many Keator relatives living in Bermuda on Cane River. As a child she visited her relatives on Cane River frequently. Lucile began boarding at St. Mary's Academy in Natchitoches when she was in seventh grade and remained there until her graduation in 1924. While at St. Mary's she became close friends with Adele Prud'homme, Alphonse's sister.

Lucile Keator and her Keator cousins picking cotton, ca 1910

When Alphonse returned to the plantation from France following the war Lucile had caught his eye. They courted and on Lucile's birthday, April 2, 1924, Alphonse surprised Lucile with an engagement ring. Alphonse and Lucile were married the following August. They raised their four children, Alphonse III, Kenneth, Mayo and Vivian at Oakland. Their marriage was one to be admired and envied.

Lucille Keator Prud'homme (1906-1994) while attending St. Mary's Academy

James Alphonse Prud'homme II (1896-1991) with his son, Alphonse III in flower garden at Oakland.

Vivian, Mayo, Kenneth, Alphonse III Prud'homme

Alphonse II followed in his father's footsteps in the management of Oakland through the mid 1900s. Cattle operations expanded but cotton was the primary crop. A portion of the Oakland store served as the farm office. In 1924 Alphonse was appointed postmaster for the Bermuda Post Office located in the store.

Cooks Cabin

The years during the Depression were lean, but the self-sufficient plantation weathered it well. Cotton and food crops continued to be grown. The cattle operation provided beef and dairy products as it had for generations. To supplement the family's income Phanor II rented cabins on the plantation for people interested in spending leisure time on Cane River. The cabin that had once served as the cook's cabin during the antebellum period adapted well as a fishing camp during the Depression. Phanor II provided boats and Alphonse II raised shiners to sell to the fishermen.

The Battle of Bermuda Bridge

The Prud'homme men were active in military affairs. The first Prud'homme, Jean Pierre Philippe, came to the new country in the 1700s as a soldier with St. Denis' French army. Alphonse I was a sergeant in the Confederate Army, Alphonse II served during World War I and Alphonse III was a sergeant in World War II. However, it was the Battle of Bermuda Bridge that brought the family national recognition.

Jacques Alphonse
Civil War,
Confederate Veteran,

Alphonse II, World War I

Alphonse III, World War II

*Cannon
Courtesy of
Mark Bills
Photography*

In September of 1941 the United States Army held maneuvers in Natchitoches Parish prior to the bombing of Pearl Harbor. While this of course was serious business, the three sons of Alphonse II and Lucile Prud'homme found the maneuvers quite entertaining. In fact, on one particular day the boys tried their skills with toy artillery. What occurred that day captured national attention. The story was later covered by The Natchitoches Times, the Times Picayune in New Orleans, Parade Magazine and even Paul Harvey. It wasn't until Paul Harvey's "The Rest of the Story" aired that the family learned that Alphonse, Ken and Mayo Prud'homme had stymied the later famous General George Patton himself.

Al, Ken and Mayo Prud'homme

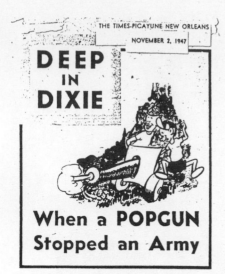

DEEP IN DIXIE

When a POPGUN Stopped an Army

Clipping from the Times Picayune, New Orleans, Louisiana. November 2, 1947

THE BATTLE of Bermuda Bridge is unlisted among history's decisive engagements but it will long be remembered as the action in which three small boys held the United States army at bay with a toy cannon.

The time was September 26, 1941, during the great army maneuvers in Central Louisiana. The place was the town of Bermuda on the Cane river. The heroes were Alphonse, Kenneth and Mayo Prudhomme, aged 14, 12 and 9 years respectively.

F. L. Hedges of Natchitoches, who tells the story of this startling military upset, writes that the Blue army was approaching Bermuda one fine fall day when it encountered the three Prudhomme boys.

"The Blue army patrol scout car," writes Mr. Hedges, "had stopped at the Bermuda store for soft drinks. There were several soldiers in the car and several others idling on the store porch. They were waiting for the main body of the Blue forces to catch up with them.

"The Prudhomme boys had a small toy cannon that shot carbide gas. The report was very loud. Just as the advancing Blue army came into view on the other side of the Bermuda bridge, the boys pointed the toy cannon across the river and opened fire. Bang!

"The advancing Blue army looked across the river and saw the scout car and the soldiers on the store porch. Thinking that they had encountered an advance guard of the Red army, instead of their own patrol car, the Blues opened fire with rifles and machine guns. This stopped the whole parade.

"The Prudhomme boys shot back at them as fast as they could load their cannon. After a while an umpire stepped out and waved his white flag for a decision. This did not stop the boys, however, and they continued to shoot. The umpire finally found out that the firing was a toy cannon and three boys. He sent word to Mrs. Prudhomme: 'Please stop your boys from shooting that cannon. They are holding up the war and most of the Blue army!' "

Hollywood Comes To Oakland Plantation

In 1958 John Ford directed the film <u>The Horse Soldiers</u> starring John Wayne, William Holden and Constance Towers. Many of the scenes for the film were shot at Oakland Plantation. Vivian Prud'homme and Jerry Cloutier were two family members participating in the cast. However, it was the Prud'homme's family dog, Whups, that commanded the highest salary for family members participating in the film.

Natchitoches Parish has hosted other films in more recent years, such as <u>Steel Magnolias</u> and <u>The Man in the Moon</u>.

Vivian Prud'homme and John Wayne

Set of Horse Soldiers at Oakland Plantation Courtesy Guillet Photography

Jerry Cloutier

Lucile, Al IV, Vivian Prud'homme with William Holden, 1958

Following Alphonse III's graduation from Northwestern State University in 1949, he entered the cotton business as a cotton buyer in Texas but he always longed to return to his home to farm the plantation. In the mid 1950s Alphonse did indeed return to Cane River to farm. His brother, Kenneth, later joined Alphonse as they continued the family tradition of farming Oakland Plantation. Alphonse II retired from farming but continued to run the plantation store.

Alphonse Prud'homme III.

James Alphonse III and Kenneth continued to farm the land well into the 1980s. Alphonse and Kenneth also observed the tradition of never working on Good Friday. Folklore among the workers suggested the "ground would bleed" if it was plowed on Good Friday. The Prud'hommes were one of the first to farm crawfish in north Louisiana although crawfishing at Oakland was purely done for pleasure and not for profit.

When Alphonse II retired from farming he enjoyed spending more time traveling with his wife, Lucile. Lucile was quite active with social and historical associations. Alphonse II would frequently accompany Lucile in her travels to various historical society conventions.

Lucile K. Prud'homme in the dining room. The punka served as a fan over the dining room table. It had a rope attached to the iron ring at the top and was pulled by one of the servants while the family was dining. The Prud'homme Coat of Arms was painted on the punka by J. Alphonse Prud'homme III.

Lucile was a great researcher and historian. She compiled and organized the Prud'homme genealogy to perfection. She was never shy about enlisting the help of her grandchildren to assist with the research. I vividly remember my twin sister and I spending hours in the cemetery with LuLu copying the names from headstones. Lucile later published a book about the cemeteries of Natchitoches Parish. Of course she would reward her grandchildren by actively involving them in her multiple historical association conventions to serve as pages or tour guides. LuLu had a remarkable talent for making her grandchildren feel important.

Pigeonnier: The pigeonniers provided a home for the pigeons used for pigeon pie and squab on toast. Square crib in back.

Alphonse II however, was more interested in reading the comic strips to his grandchildren. My fondest memories were of visiting "Paw Paw" at the store where he kept an enormous "Jack's Cookie" jar on the counter. He had the magical talent of always finding nickels in his grandchildren's ears so that we had just enough money to purchase a cookie or two. Alphonse and Lucile lived to share their lives with many of their great grandchildren.

Negotiations with the National Park Service began in the 1980s. Alphonse died in 1991 and Lucile in 1994. Paw Paw's tales of how the plantation was when he was a boy motivated the family more towards the dream of restoring the plantation to its once grand splendor. A granddaughter, Denise Poleman and her family lived in the home during the final negotiations with the National Park Service representing the 7th and 8th generations of Prud'hommes to live at Oakland Plantation. Approximately 41 acres including the Big House and 14 outbuildings became part of the Cane River Creole National Historical Park in 1997.

Mule Barn, formerly the smokehouse

Chicken coops

Lucile Keator, bride of J. Alphonse Prud'homme, August 9, 1924.

LIFESTYLES ALONG *LA COTE JOYEUSE*

Weddings and Anniversaries

Typical within the nineteenth century Creole culture was the intermarrying of cousins. This was a tightly knit social group and any prospective suitor had to pass family scrutiny before *entre de la maison*. It was preferred that the suitor be well bred *"c'est un gentil garcon."* Occasionally the French Creoles of Natchitoches courted other Creoles from predominantly French areas, such as New Orleans, but geographically it was simpler to court locally. Therefore it was not unusual to find two or three siblings of one family marrying two or three siblings of another family. A close review of the Prud'homme family tree will reveal frequent intermarrying with the Lambres, Cloutiers and Breazeales, as well as other Prud'hommes.

The ceremonies were usually grand including a Roman Catholic Nuptial Mass and reception at the bride's home. It was also customary to celebrate anniversaries in elaborate style. While most Prud'homme weddings occurred in Catholic churches, scores of wedding receptions were held at Oakland. Documentation reveals that many workers were married on the Oakland grounds. Two weddings that occurred in the parlor of Oakland Plantation were those of Maie Prud'homme to Robert Hunter in 1903 and my own marriage to G. Michael Haynie, M.D. in 1996.

When Catherine Adeline Prud'homme married Winter Wood Breazeale in 1856, the groom presented his fiance with a *corbeille de marriage* he ordered from Paris. *Corbeille* is French for basket. Winter Wood presented the wedding gift to Catherine Adeline prior to the ceremony. The gleaming ebony box was inlaid with mother of pearl and gold engravings. Inside were a wedding veil, ivory stick fan, French kid gloves, a wedding handkerchief, small slippers, a prayer book and rosary and her second day dress. Over the years the *corbeille* and its treasures have been passed down to descendants of Catherine Adeline.[19]

Elisa Elizabeth Prud'homme (bride of Wilbur Guy Cloutier June 10, 1925) Courtesy Mr. and Mrs. Arnold Cloutier

Three fiftieth wedding anniversaries were celebrated at Oakland Plantation. Jacques Alphonse I and Elisa Lecomte Prud'homme celebrated their anniversary in 1914.

---

[19] Attributed to Mary Breazeale Cunningham, descendant of Catherine Adeline Prud'homme Breazeale, who wrote the story in 1958 while a journalism student at Louisiana State University

Pierre Phanor and his wife Laura Cloutier at the time of their 50th wedding anniversary in 1941.

The event began with Mass at St. Charles Chapel in Bermuda, Louisiana. Specially chartered trains delivered guests to Oakland Plantation from New Orleans and Shreveport. These trains were held on sidetracks at a small station at Brevelle between Cypress and Natchez, Louisiana. The famous Gruenwald Hotel from New Orleans provided catering and a New Orleans orchestra provided the music for dancing. With the approach of dawn the out of town guests were taken to their respective trains thus ending the festivities.

Pierre Phanor and Laure Cloutier Prud'homme celebrated their fiftieth anniversary in 1941. Alex Cloutier sang "Dearest, How I Love You," just as he had sung it at their wedding fifty years earlier.

I remember my grandparents' fiftieth anniversary celebration like it was yesterday. I was just a teenager but all of the grandchildren, even the youngest ones, were able to attend the gala event. James Alphonse Prud'homme II and Lucile Keator Prud'homme, better known as Paw Paw and LuLu, celebrated the event in style. I especially recall my younger brother, Michael, sneaking a bit of champagne and feeling quite ill the following day.

Two of Elisa Prud'homme Cloutier's children celebrated a double wedding with the reception being held at Oakland July 29, 1951.

Pictured Front (bottom) row: Paul Legrand, Marie Cloutier Legrand, Pete Deffes, Virginia LeMeur Cloutier and Arnold Cloutier. 2nd row: Ethlyn Cloutier, Gordon Collins, Jane Allen (Prud'homme). 3rd row: Amelie Cloutier, Layton Stephenson, Susie Bishop. 4th row: Jackie Legrand, Tilton Mallerich, Vivian Prud'homme, Lorraine LeMeur 5th row: Kathleen Prud'homme, Maurice Legrand, Adeline Gaiennie. Back row: Kenneth Prud'homme

Anne Prud'homme Aviles dancing with her father, Kenneth
Prud'homme during her wedding reception at Oakland in 1995.
Courtesy Mr. & Mrs. Kenneth Prud'homme

Sandra Prud'homme and G. Michael Haynie M.D. in the parlor during
their wedding in 1996. Reverend Pat Day presiding.
Courtesy Guillet Photography

Cane River

Cane River Ferry

Cane River once was a part of the Red River, which was a primary source of transportation in Louisiana for centuries. Originally the plantation covered lands on both sides of the river. Even after the Red River changed its course in the 1830s, the old course of the river, now called Cane River Lake, still carried a lot of steamboat traffic. There was once an official steamboat landing at Oakland Plantation. According to my grandfather, James Alphonse Prud'homme II, the waterway still was a valuable source of transportation in the early 1900s.

There is no disputing the fact that the Cane River is incredibly crooked. My grandfather would tell the story of the night the Lord mapped the river. Legend has it that on a particularly stormy night the Lord's only source of light was from the lighting. Each time lightening would strike the Lord would move His pen. He continued mapping the river despite the storm. As a result the Cane River was quite crooked. The next morning the Lord looked at the map and found it too much trouble to straighten the river.

Over the years many a steamboat captain lamented the Lord's decision not to straighten the river. My grandfather would tell stories of how as a young lad in the early 1900's he would see the steamboats in the distance heading toward the plantation. He and his siblings loved to greet the steamboats. They would hear the whistle, see the smokestack and wait sometimes an hour for the steamboat's arrival.

Cane River was dammed in 1936 creating Cane River Lake. Cane River not only provided transportation it greatly influenced the Bermuda social circle for many years. Swimming, fishing and in later generations, water skiing were enjoyed.

Cane River after the Bermuda bridge was completed in 1912. View from the East Bank looking at the West Bank, slave cabins at Oakland.

Swimming was also enjoyed at Kisatchie: Front row: Mildred Hill, Celia Morse, Sam Hill, Jr. 2nd row: Sam Hill, Sr. holding Cora Lee Hill, Ruth Raggio, Lallah Prud'homme Hill, Norma Hill. Back row: Cookie. Courtesy Mildred "Mimi" Methvin.

Religion

The Prud'hommes were devout Catholics. The Catholic religion was such a dominant force in the Prud'homme family, even the workers were baptized. Female members attended the Ursuline Convent in New Orleans during the early 1800s. Lestan Prud'homme's diary of the 1850s mentions the female members of the Prud'homme family also attended Sacred Heart Convent in Natchitoches. Apparently the girls boarded at the convent and Lestan always looked forward to their return to the plantation during breaks.

After the Civil War the Daughters of the Cross experienced difficult times and Sacred Heart Convent closed. In the late 1800s some of Jacques Alphonse's daughters boarded at St. Vincent's Academy in Shreveport, Louisiana and the sons attended the University of Notre Dame. By the early 1900s the Sisters of Divine Providence opened St. Mary's Academy where other Prud'homme children attended.

St Mary's Academy, Natchitoches, Louisiana
Courtesy Roland Achee

Sister Corine's 5th & 6th grades at St Marys circa 1942: Including Agnes Culpepper, Mary Gunn, Mildred Methvin, Mayo Prud'homme, John Cunningham, Robert "Bobby" DeBlieux, Alton Hernandez, Kathy Prud'homme and Charles Prud'homme

Confirmation: Kenneth Prud'homme, Wilbur Cloutier, Marie Cloutier and James Alphonse Prud'homme III, circa 1941.

Altar Boys: Top Row L to R: Giles Millspaugh, Lucian Rogers. Alfred Ducournau, Henry Breazeale, John Payne, Titus Frederick, Vernon Cloutier
4th Row: Emmanuel Cloutier, Edwin Davis, Edwin Dranguet, Leslie Babbin, Father Piegay, Sam Hill, Vienne (Boone) Trichel, Ed Payne, Vernon Cook
3rd Row: Richard DeVargus, Reynolds Bath, unknown, Ross Maggio, J.H. Williams, Jack Ducournau, Preston Smith, John Cunningham, Edmond Hawkins
2nd Row: Lawrence Perini, Nord Smith, Clarence Tauzin, Louis Bowsher, Raymond Breazeale, Clyde Vienne
1st Row: Leslie Prud'homme, Earl Cook, Hardy Blanchard, unknown, Murphy Collins, Ambrose Lecomte Dranguet, George Breazeale.   Circa 1915
Courtesy David Williamson

St. Charles Chapel
From the early 1900s to
recent times the family
attended St. Charles Chapel
in Bermuda, Louisiana.

*Adeline Prudhomme Cloutier
(Reared at Ataho, living at
Oaklawn Plantation at
time of photo, 1960s)
St. Charles Chapel*

Beth Cloutier (Beau Fort Plantation), Cleo Dranguet, Edgar Cloutier, Judy Dranguet, Ted Duggan, and children, Michael, Renee, Kathy and Sandra Prud'homme, circa 1964, St. Charles Chapel

Catherine Adeline Prud'homme, First Communion, circa 1969 at St. Charles Chapel

Josie Breazeale, Kathleen Prud'homme Batten, Kenneth, Jane and Lucile Prud'homme, Beth Cloutier, Joanne Breazeale Gardner and Cissy Breazeale Cunningham, circa 1959

Sandra Prud'homme, Daisy Prud'homme, Retta Lambre Cloutier, Ethelyn Cloutier, circa 1964, St. Charles Chapel

Christening of Zachary Quiros, son of Renee Prud'homme Quiros, 1997. Left to Right: Dylan Payne, Mike Haynie, Mayo and Annette Prud'homme, Lawton and Keator Poleman, Judith Prud'homme, Eugene Flores, Julie Prud'homme, Kenneth, Vivian and Cappy Prud'homme, Terry Guin, Sally Prud'homme, Ken Poleman, Kathy Guin, Dick Williamson, Jane Prud'homme DeBlieux, Michael and Lisa Prud'homme and Dylan Williams. St. Charles Chapel, Courtesy Renee Prud'homme Quiros, photography by John C. Guillet.

Sportsman's Paradise on the Plantation

Hunting was avidly enjoyed by most of the Prud'hommes. Snipe, doves, duck, squirrel, rabbit, deer and even opossum were hunted on Oakland Plantation. Fishing on Cane River and crawfishing in the pond were also pursued.

Reference to hunting on the place is found in Lestan Prud'homme's diary following the Mardi Gras of 1850. Lestan Prud'homme visited Phanor and Lise Metoyer Prud'homme at Oakland. The diary reads in part:

> *Tuesday-19th*
>
> *...I intended this day to resume my studies I had left last week, and was about getting to work when Mrs. Valery, accompanied by Felix, arrived here; the former to spend the day, and the latter with all his hunting instruments ready to go snipe hunting. Being invited by him to participate in the sport the day being beautiful and the idea of going to shoot snipes again took me from my studies. In a moment the horse was saddled, I was as soon ready and off, both of us went anticipating a glorious hunt. Unfortunately, contrary to our expectations, we found but very few, and very wild snipes; I had the good luck of killing eight or nine but my companion was entirely disgusted, not having been able to shoot more than once or twice.*
>
> *We got back at Phanor's after the dinner was over, but the table was soon set, and after partaking of a good dinner we were treated with two or three dozen of fine oysters.[20]*

---

[20] Lestan Prudhomme diary, 1850-1852, Irma Sompayrac Willard Collection, Cammie Henry Research Center, Northwestern State University, Natchitoches, La (original in Howard-Tilton Memorial Library, Tulane University, New Orleans). *Courtesy Dan Willard*

Alphonse II and his brother in law, Jesse Brett, prepare for a hunt in 1932

Dylan Payne, son of Sandra Prud'homme Haynie, 1982

James Alphonse Prud'homme II and Reginald Prud'homme

The Bermuda Tennis Club

As early as 1891 the Bermuda community had organized a tennis club. The tennis courts were on the front lawn of Oakland Plantation. Members of the 1891 tennis club were E. G. Lawton M.D. (Pres.), Valsin Lambre (V.Pres.), Cora Prud'homme (Treas.), Lise Prud'homme (Secretary), Edward C. Prud'homme, Phanor Prud'homme, Felix Prud'homme, James Prud'homme, Wilmer Breazeale, J. Alphonse Prud'homme, Placide Prud'homme, Lambre Prud'homme, Ailhaud Prud'homme, Ovide Prud'homme, Sidney Cloutier, Edgar Cloutier, W.W. Breazeale, Jr., Walter Breazeale, Alain Metoyer, Octave Lambre, Emanuel Buard, B.B. Breazeale M.D., P.E. Prud'homme.

Tennis continued to be played at Oakland for the next two generations.

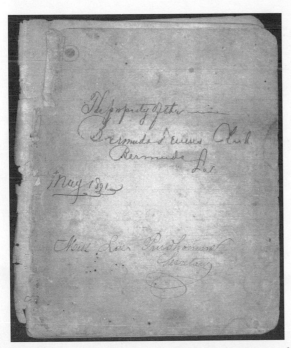

Minutes kept by Lise Prud'homme, secretary of the Bermuda Tennis Club, 1891. Courtesy Northwestern State University of Louisiana, Watson Memorial Library, Cammie G. Henry Research Center, David Williamson Collection.

Lucile and Alphonse Prud'homme after a tennis match at Oakland, 1925. Courtesy Doris Ann Brett Vincent

Adele Prud'homme after a tennis match at Oakland, 1925. Courtesy Doris Ann Brett Vincent

The Annual Historic Tour

As long as I can remember there has been an annual fall tour of homes, a function of the Association for the Preservation of Historic Natchitoches, in Natchitoches and along Cane River. As a young girl it was always a treat to dress-up in antebellum attire and greet the tourists during cotton harvest season. The ladies primarily wore calico dresses over hoop-skirts and the younger girls wore dresses over pantaloons. I recall the scent of defoliant lingering in the air from the cotton fields as well as an occasional whiff of the sweet olive blooming in the garden. The spider lilies would be in bloom bordering the brick walk to Oakland's entrance.

The plantation was a beehive of activity as my grandmother, Lucile Prud'homme, spearheaded the event at Oakland. I was probably about 8 years old when I was able to volunteer for the annual affair.

Vivian and Lucile Prud'homme in the Dining room admiring Portrait of Jean Pierre Emmanuel Prud'homme. The books in the old bookcase were printed between 1800 and 1825. Most are first editions and printed in French.

1956 Tour at Oakland; left to right
Ethelyn Cloutier, Kathleen Prud'homme, Doris Ann Brett, Lucie Prud'homme, Lucile
Keator Prud'homme, Mildred Hill Cunningham, Adele Prud'homme Brett, Amelie
Cloutier, Mary Leonie Prud'homme, Daisy Prud'homme, Vivian Prud'homme. Courtesy
Doris Ann Vincent

Vivian Prud'homme with tack, circa 1958   Cora "Dootsie" Baker circa 1959

Mildred Hill Cunningham with silver service (St. Charles Hotel Trophy) won by Ambrose Lecomte's racehorse, The Flying Dutchman, circa 1850 at the Metarie Race Track, now the Metarie Cemetary. Borrowed from Magnolia Plantation for the tour (circa 1959)

Front: Kathy and Sandra Prud'homme and Suzette Cloutier.
Back: Jane Prud'homme, Sandy Bolton, Jan Sullivan and Ethelyn Cloutier, circa 1965.

Carmen Breazeale presenting Lucile Keator Prud'homme with citation from the "Association of Natchitoches Women for the Preservation of Historic Natchitoches," now known as the APHN. Also: Mrs. James Alphonse Prud'homme III, with twin daughters, Kathy and Sandra Prud'homme in calico dresses worn for the tour in 1966, Oakland Plantation.

Denise, Andrea and Eugene Flores in the parlor 1968

Kathy, Renee and Sandra Prud'homme, Oakland Fall Tour 1968

Lisa Prud'homme 1995. Courtesy Michael Prud'homme

Sarah Blanchard, great granddaughter of Laura Prud'homme,
Greeting tourist, circa 1995

Karen Lindeman and Colleen Barton, Granddaughters of Adele
Prud'homme Brett (1995) Courtesy Karen Lindeman

Amanda and Bridget Winder on the gallery, great-granddaughters of
Alphonse and Lucile Prud'homme, circa 1995. Courtesy Denise Poleman

Karen Lindeman and Kathleen Prud'homme Batten, 1995 in the dining room: The calendar clock was made in St. Louis using Seth Thomas works about 1876. It still runs and automatically adjusts for leap year.

Kenneth, Jr. "Drew," Cappy, Sally, and Kenneth, Sr. Prud'homme, circa 1995

Christmas at Oakland Plantation

Christmas at Oakland was magical. The season began with the Natchitoches Christmas Festival. Meat pies, gumbo, parades, fireworks and Midnight Mass were just a few of the traditions enjoyed by the family during the season. Several Prud'homme descendants won the title of Miss Merry Christmas or Christmas Belle.

Scott Payne, son of Sandra Prud'homme, intrigued by the Christmas village 1983

Front row L to R: Sandra, Kathy, Alphonse II and Cappy Prud'homme, Denise Flores, Lucile and Al IV Prud'homme and Andrea Flores
Second row: Michael and Renee Prud'homme and Eugene Flores
Third row: Jane, Al III, Kenneth, Sally, Mayo I, Mayo II, Annette, Julie Prud'homme, Vivian and Eugene Flores. 1966
Courtesy Guillet Photography

Marietta Baker, granddaughter of Lallah Prud'homme Hill, as Miss Merry Christmas 1960.

Lisa Cloutier, granddaughter of Lisa Prud'homme Cloutier, on the gallery at Oakland, Miss Merry Christmas 1975. Lisa also held the title of Louisiana Junior Miss.

GENEALOGY

The Prud'homme Family Tree

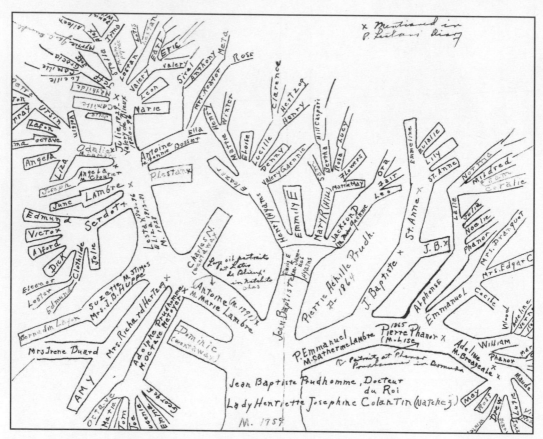

Irma Sompayrac Willard's sketch of the Prud'homme Family Tree

PRUD'HOMME GENERATIONS

1ST GENERATION IN AMERICA

Husband's full name: *Jean Pierre Philippe Prud'homme*
- Birth: *ca 1673, Romans Dauphine, France*
- Death: *Jan. 22, 1739, Natchitoches, La*
- Occupation: *Soldier French Army*
- His Father: *Pierre Prud'homme (France)*
- His Mother: *Bruchard (France)*
- Church: *Catholic*

Wife's full name: *Marie Catherine Meslier Picard*
- Birth: *ca.1705 Paris, France*
- Death: *Oct. 11, 1781, Natchitoches, La*
- 2nd Marriage: *Pierre Allargearge (1741)*

Children:

Pierre Emmanuel Prud'homme
- Birth: *1726, Natchitoches, La*
- Death: *1767*

Jean Francois Prud'homme
- Birth: *Dec. 20, 1727, Natchitoches, La.*
- Marriage: *M. Barbara Rambin, May 9, 1780, Natchitoches, La.*
- Death: *1823*

Pierre Prud'homme
- Birth: *1729, Natchitoches, La*
- Marriage: *Madeline Bouchard, Jan. 9, 1753, Natchitoches, La.*
- Death: *1767*

Pierre Sebastien Prud'homme

Birth: *Sep. 10, 1733, Natchitoches, La.*
Marriage: *M. Jeane Chevert, Jan. 8, 1752, Natchitoches, La.*
Death: *Jan 9, 1787, Natchitoches, Louisiana*

Marguerite Victorie Prud'homme

Birth: *1736, Natchitoches, La*
Marriage: *Pierre Tristant, Nov. 8, 1752, Natchitoches, La.*
2nd Marriage: *Elennie Ternie*
3rd Marriage: *Pierre Durrant*
Death: *Oct. 2, 1813, Natchitoches, La.*

Jean Baptiste Prud'homme, M.D.
(Docteur du Roi)

Birth: *ca 1735, Natchitoches, La.*
1st Marriage: *Marie Chevert 1756*
2nd Marriage: *M. Josephine H. Collantine (Corantine), July 13, 1758, Natchitoches, La.*
Death: *Oct. 20, 1786, Natchitoches, La.*

Marie Prud'homme

Birth: *ca 1738, Natchitoches, La.*
(Godparents: St. Denis & wife)
Death: *Unknown*

Ed Prud'homme, member of the 1953 football team at the University of Notre Dame.

Husband's full name: *Jean Baptist Prud'homme*
    Birth: *1735, Natchitoches, La.*
    Marriage: *M. Josephine H. Collantine (Corantine)*
    July 13, 1758, Natchitoches, La.
    Death: *Oct. 20, 1786, Natchitoches, La.*
    Occupation: *Medical doctor*
    Church: *Catholic*
    His Father: *Jean P. Philippe Prud'homme*
    His Mother: *M. Catherine Picard*

Wife's full name: *Marie Joseph Francoise Charlotte H.*
    Collantine (Corantine)
    Birth: *1738, New Orleans, La.*
    Death: *Feb. 16, 1788, Natchitoches, La.*

Children:
    Jean Baptiste Prud'homme
    Birth: *1759, Natchitoches, La.*
    Death: *Unknown*

    Marie Louise Prud'homme
    Birth: *Nov. 9, 1760, Natchitoches, La.*
    Marriage: *Francois Rouquier, May 5, 1782,*
    Natchitoches, La.
    Death: *Unknown*

Opelousas, Louisiana. Former Plantation of Jean-Michel Prud'homme (circa 1737-1817), a native of Strasbourg, Alsace, France.

Jean Pierre Emmanuel Prud'homme
Builder of Bermuda (Oakland) Plantation

Birth: Jan. 2, 1762, Natchitoches, La.
Marriage: M. Catherine Lambre, Jan. 7, 1784, Natchitoches, La.
Death: May 13, 1845, Natchitoches, La.

Antoine Prud'homme

Birth: Nov. 9, 1764, Natchitoches, La.
Marriage: M. Jacques Lambre, Aug. 31, 1791, Natchitoches, La.
Death: Aug. 18, 1856, Natchitoches, La.

Dominique Prud'homme

Birth: Feb. 5, 1767, Natchitoches, La.
Death: Left home – never returned

Anna Nanette Prud'homme

Birth: Dec. 17, 1768, Natchitoches, La.
Marriage: Phillipe William Benjamin Gilles DuParc,
Mar. 17, 1788, New Orleans, La.
Death: 1862, DuParc Plantation

Susanne Prud'homme

Birth: Jun. 17, 1775, Natchitoches, La.
Marriage: Remy Lambre, Sep. 24, 1789, Natchitoches, La.
Death: April 10, 1815, Natchitoches, La.

Francois Prud'homme

Birth: May 15, 1777, Natchitoches, La.
Death: ca 1798, Natchitoches, La.

*Marie Eliza (Eleysa) (Laiza) Lambre (1813-1881), Daughter of
Susanne Prud'homme and Remy Lambre. Wife of J.J. Lestan
Prud'homme. Niece of Catherine Lambre Prud'homme, builder of
Oakland. Courtesy Conna Cloutier*

*Tante Huppe House. Home belonged to Suzette "Tante Huppe"
Prud'homme Lafon LeComte Huppe, daughter of Antoine Prud'homme.
Diarist, Lestan Prud'homme lived with his Tante Huppe for a while.
Home presently owned by a descendant, Robert "Bobby" DeBlieux*

Mary Keator, Cyril Prud'homme, Anthony Prud'homme, Meda Keator, Rose Keator, Bermuda, Louisiana, circa 1909.

Lestan Prud'homme and Lucille Cloutier

Husband's full name: *Jean Pierre Emmanuel Prud'homme*
  Birth: *Jan. 2, 1762, Natchitoches, La*
  Marriage: *M.Catherine Lambre, Jan. 7, 1784,*
         Natchitoches, La.
  Death: *May 13, 1845, Natchitoches, La.*
  Occupation: *Builder of Oakland (Bermuda) Plantation*
  Church: *Catholic*
  His Father: *Jean Baptiste Prud'homme*
  His Mother: *M. Joseph Francoise Charlotte H. Corantin (Collantin)*

Wife's maiden name: *Marie Catherine Lambre*
  Birth: *1763, Natchitoches, La.*
  Death: *Aug. 4, 1848, Natchitoches, La.*

Children:

  Pierre Emmanuel Jean Baptiste Prud'homme
  Birth: *Jun. 23, 1785, Natchitoches, La.*
  Marriage: *M. Therese Victorie Ailhaud St. Anne, Oct. 10, 1806,*
         Natchitoches, La.
  Death: *Aug. 17, 1861, Natchitoches, La.*

  Henriette Prud'homme
  Birth: *1786, Natchitoches, La.*
  Marriage: *Dr. Englass,1806, Natchitoches, La.*
  Death: *Unknown*

  Louis Narcisse Prud'homme
  Birth: *Aug. 24, 1788, Natchitoches, La.*
  Marriage: *Marie Therese Elizabeth Metoyer, Sep. 23, 1806,*
         Natchitoches, La.
  Death: *Mar. 25, 1844, Natchitoches, La.*

Marie Adele Prud'homme (twin)

Birth: *Nov. 14, 1800, Natchitoches, La.*

Marriage: *Jean Baptiste Lecomte, Dec. 22, 1814, Natchitoches, La.*

Death: *Dec. 26, 1815 (In childbirth) Natchitoches, La.*

Marie Adeline Prud'homme (twin)

Birth: *Nov. 14, 1800, Natchitoches, La.*

Marriage: *Jean Francois Roques, Jan. 1818, New Orleans, La.*

Death: *Oct. 27, 1878, Nantes, France*

Pierre Phanor Prud'homme I

Birth: *Jun. 24, 1807, Natchitoches, La.*

1st Marriage: *Susanne Lise Metoyer, Jan. 12, 1835, Isle Brevelle, Natchitoches, La.*

2nd Marriage: *M. Cephalide Archinard Metoyer*

Death: *Oct. 12, 1865, Natchitoches, La.*

Infant Prud'homme

Birth: *Nov. 1798, Natchitoches, La.*

Death: *Nov. 25, 1798, Natchitoches, La.*

Infant

Birth:

Death: *Oct. 6, 1803, Natchitoches, La.*

Ursin Lambre, husband of Emma Breazeale (daughter of Henriette Prud'homme Breazeale) Courtesy Conna Cloutier

Cedar Bend Plantation. Legend claims the plantation was spared during the Civil War because the Creole family displayed the French flag indicating French citizenship as the Union Army passed. The home has belonged to descendants of Emmanuel Prud'homme of Oakland Plantation for generations. Currently John E. Prud'homme, son of Dr. J. Hebert Prud'homme, and his wife Maxine own the home.

Joseph Hebert Prud'homme, DDS (1880-1946), son of Josephine Cecile Buard (1848-1938) and Joseph Ailhaud Prud'homme (1845-1920). Joseph Ailhaud Prud'homme was the son of Gabriel Ailhaud St. Anne Prud'homme (1808-1865) and Marie Aglae Prud'homme (1812-1901). Gabriel Ailhaud St. Anne Prud'homme (1808-1865) was the son of Jean Baptiste Prud'homme II (1785-1861) and Marie Therese Victoire Ailhaud de St. Anne. Marie Aglae Prud'homme (1812-1901) was the daughter of Narcisse Prud'homme I and Marie Therese Elizabeth Metoyer.

Husband's full name: *Pierre Phanor Prud'homme*
    Birth: *Jun. 24, 1807, Natchitoches, La.*

    Marriage: *1st Wife – Susanne Lise Metoyer, Jan 12, 1835, Isle Brevelle, Louisiana*

    2nd Wife - Marianne Cephalide Metoyer Archinard
    Death: *Oct. 12, 1865, Natchitoches, La.*
    Occupation: *Planter*
    Church: *Catholic*
    His Father: *Jean Pierre Emmanuel Prud'homme*
    His Mother: *M. Catherine Lambre*

Wife's maiden name: *Susanne Lise Metoyer*
    Birth: *Nov. 22, 1818, Metoyer Point Plantation, La.*
    Marriage: *Pierre Phanor Prud'homme*
    Death: *May 19, 1852, Oakland Plantation*

Children:

    Catherine Adeline Prud'homme
    Birth: *Mar. 6, 1836, Natchitoches, La.*
    Marriage: *Winter Wood Breazeale, Jan. 16, 1856 Natchitoches,La.*
    Death: *Oct. 27, 1878, Natchitoches, La.*

    Jacques Alphonse Prud'homme
    Birth: *Apr. 17, 1838, Natchitoches, La.*
    Marriage: *Elisa E. Lecomte, Sep. 6, 1864, Natchitoches, La.*
    Death: *Feb. 17, 1919, Bermuda, La.*

Marie Emma Prud'homme

Birth: Aug. 11, 1839, Natchitoches, La.
Death: Oct. 4, 1854, Natchitoches, La.

Marie Therese Henriette Prud'homme

Birth: May. 26, 1842, Natchitoches, La.
Marriage: Dr. Blount Baker Breazeale, Jr., Feb. 28, 1865, Natchitoches,La.
Death: Apr. 19, 1922, Natchitoches, Louisiana

Pierre Emmanuel Prud'homme

Birth: Jan. 8, 1844, Natchitoches, La.
Marriage: Marie Julie Buard, Jan. 25, 1866, Natchitoches, La.
Death: Apr. 10, 1934, Natchitoches, La.

Julia Buard LeComte (1809-1845); mother of Elisa LeComte Prud'homme Courtesy Betty Hertzog, Magnolia Plantation

Mrs. Jean Louis Buard (nee Eulalie Bossier) (1781-1836); Maternal grand-mother of Elisa LeComte Prud'homme Courtesy Conna Cloutier

Pierre Emmanuel Prud'homme (1844-1934) and wife, Julia Buard Courtesy Kathleen Prud'homme Batten

4 generations (circa 1930) back steps of Ataho Plantation:
Front: Baby-Daisy Marguerite Prud'homme (1930-   )
2nd row: Louise Desiree Cloutier Prud'homme (1897- 1981)
           Francis Reginald Prud'homme (1900-1967)
3rd row: Emma Laura Buard Prud'homme (1873-1972)
           Edward Carrington Prud'homme (1869-1941)
4th row: Julie Buard Prud'homme (1845-1934)
           Pierre Emmanuel Prud'homme (1844-1934)
Courtesy Kathleen Prud'homme Batten

Husband's full name: *Jacques Alphonse Prud'homme*
    Birth: *Apr. 17, 1838, Natchitoches, La.*
    Marriage: *Elisa Elizabeth Lecomte, Sep. 6, 1864,*
                         Natchitoches, La.
    Death: *Feb. 17, 1919, Natchitoches, La.*
    Occupation: *Planter*
    Military: *Civil War*
    Church: *Catholic*
    His Father: *Pierre Phanor Prud'homme*
    His Mother: *Susanne Lise Metoyer*

Wife's maiden name: *Elisa Elizabeth LeComte*
    Birth: *Nov. 19, 1840, Natchitoches, La.*
    Marriage: *Jacques Alphonse Prud'homme 1864*
    Death: *Oct. 20, 1923, Natchitoches, La.*

Children:

                 Pierre Phanor Prud'homme
    Birth: *Sep. 18, 1865, Natchitoches, La.*
    Marriage: *Marie Laure Cloutier, Feb. 3, 1891,*
                         Natchitoches, La.
    Death: *May 21, 1948, Natchitoches, La.*

                 Jules Lecomte Prud'homme
    Birth: *Jun. 26, 1867, Natchitoches, La.*
    Death: *Oct. 5, 1916, Natchitoches, La.*

Edward Carrington Prud'homme

Birth: *Jul. 12, 1869, Natchitoches, La.*
Marriage: *E. Laura Prud'homme, Oct. 17, 1894,*
Natchitoches, La.
Death: *Feb. 5, 1941, Natchitoches, La.*

Marie Cora Prud'homme

Birth: *Oct. 20, 1871, Natchitoches, La.*
Marriage: *Edward G. Lawton, Aug. 7, 1894, Natchitoches, La.*
Death: *Jan. 8, 1952, Natchitoches, La.*

Marie Atala "Lallah" Prud'homme

Birth: *Sep. 25, 1875, Natchitoches, La.*
Marriage: *Samuel Hyams Hill, Apr. 26, 1898, Natchitoches, La.*
Death: *May 23, 1958, Natchitoches, La.*

Julia Eleanore Prud'homme

Birth: *Feb. 15, 1878, Natchitoches, La.*
Death: *Jan. 30, 1933, Natchitoches, La.*

Marie Maie Prud'homme

Birth: *Jun. 7, 1880, Natchitoches, La.*
Marriage: *Robert A. Hunter, Jun. 30, 1903, Natchitoches, La.*
Death: *Nov. 16, 1964, Shreveport, La.*

Marie Noelie Prud'homme

Birth: *Dec. 26, 1883, Natchitoches, La.*
Marriage: *Dr. Leroy Cockfield, Apr. 23, 1917, Natchitoches, La.*
Death: *Jun. 4, 1978, Natchitoches, La.*

*Noelie Prud'homme (1883-1978) and Norma Hill at Oakland
(store in background)
Courtesy Cammie Henry Research Center, Northwestern State
University, Natchitoches. La., Henley Hunter Collection*

Visiting Pike's Peak Cog Road
Front Row: J. Alphonse Prud'homme I and Matthew Hertzog
Back Row: Elisa LeComte Prud'homme, Noelie Prud'homme
and Atla Hertzog (Elisa's Sister)

Husband's full name: *Pierre Phanor Prud'homme*
   Birth: *Sep. 18, 1865, Natchitoches, La.*
   Marriage: *M. Laure Cloutier, Feb. 3, 1891, Natchitoches, La.*
   Death: *May 21, 1948, Natchitoches, La.*
   Church: *Catholic*
   Occupation: *Farmer*
   His Father: *J. Alphonse Prud'homme*
   His Mother: *Elise E. Lecomte*

Wife's maiden name: *Marie Laure Cloutier*
   Birth: *Jan. 25, 1871, Natchitoches, La.*
   Death: *Dec. 31, 1941, Bermuda, La.*

Children:

   James Alphonse Prud'homme
   Birth: *Dec. 28, 1896, Natchitoches (Oakland), La.*
   Marriage: *Rosalie Lucile Keator, Aug. 9, 1924, Webster Groves ,St. Louis, Missouri*
   Death: *Oct. 3, 1991*

   Louise Vivian Prud'homme
   Birth: *Feb. 9, 1899, Oakland Plantation, Bermuda, La.*
   Death: *Mar. 29, 1905, Oakland Plantation, Bermuda, La.*

   Elisa Elizabeth Prud'homme
   Birth: *Dec. 12, 1900, Oakland Plantation, Bermuda, La.*
   Marriage: *Wilbur Guy Coutier, Jun. 20, 1925, Bermuda, La.*
   Death: *Oct. 1953, Shreveport, Louisiana*

   Marie Adele Prud'homme
   Birth: *Mar. 3, 1903, Oakland Plantation, Bermuda, La.*
   Marriage: *Jesse Emmett Brett, Sep. 1, 1932, Bermuda, La.*
   Death: *Feb. 20,1974, Bermuda, La.*

Marie Leanore Prud'homme

Birth: *Apr. 16, 1905, Oakland Plantation, Bermuda, La.*

Death: *May 27, 1905, Oakland Plantation, Bermuda, La.*
(buried in Natchitoches, La.)

Pierre Phanor Prud'homme

Birth: *Feb. 17, 1908, Oakland Plantation, Bermuda, La.*

Death: *Feb. 28, 1908, Oakland Plantation, Bermuda, La.*

Pierre Phanor Prud'homme

Birth: *Jan. 26, 1909, Oakland Plantation, Bermuda, La.*

Death: *Sep. 20, 1979, Natchitoches, La.*

Marie Lucie Prud'homme

Birth: *May 25, 1911, Oakland Plantation, Bermuda, La.*

Death: *Feb. 9, 1976, Natchitoches, La.*

Louis Donald Prud'homme

Birth: *Aug. 30, 1913, Oakland Plantation, Bermuda, La.*

Death: *March 21, 1993*

Mary Keator Breazeale feeding chickens

Husband's full name: *James Alphonse Prud'homme II*

Birth:	*Dec. 28, 1896, Bermuda, Natchitoches, La.*
Marriage:	*Rosalie Lucile Keator, Aug. 9, 1924, Webster Groves, St. Louis, Missouri*
Death:	*Oct. 3, 1991*
Occupation:	*Farmer*
Military:	*WWI*
Church:	*Catholic*
His Father:	*Pierre Phanor Prud'homme*
His Mother:	*M. Laure Cloutier*

Wife's maiden name: *Rosalie Lucile Keator*

Birth:	*Apr. 2, 1906, Webster Groves, St. Louis, Missouri*
Death:	*Sept. 1, 1994*

Children:

James Alphonse Prud'homme, III

Birth:	*1927, Bermuda, Natchitoches, La.*
Marriage:	*Martha Jane Allen, Sep. 9, 1951, Pine Prairie, La.*
Death:	*Jun. 13, 1988, VA Hospital, Alexandria, La.*

Kenneth Andrew Prud'homme

Birth:	*1929, Bermuda, Natchitoches, Louisiana*
Marriage:	*Sally Anne Calhoun, Nov. 9, 1958, Colfax, La.*

Mayo Keator Prud'homme

Birth:	*1932, Bermuda, Natchitoches, Louisiana*
Marriage:	*Annette Berry, Mar. 24, 1963, Bastrop, La.*

Rose Vivian Prud'homme

Birth:	*1934, Bermuda, Natchitoches, La.*
1st Marriage:	*Eugene Joseph Flores, Apr. 23, 1960, Natchitoches, La.*
2nd Marriage:	*Ted Edward Duggan, Feb. 13, 1999, Bermuda, La.*

Lucile Keator Prud'homme
(1906-1994)

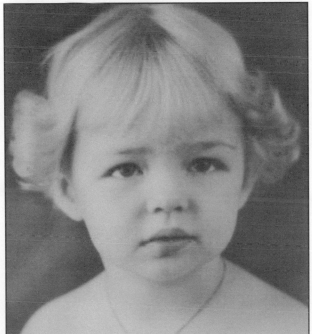

Vivian Prud'homme (1934-)

Mayo (Meullion) Sands Keator (1869-1955)
father of Lucile Prud'homme

Mable Blake Keator (1876-1955)
mother of Lucile Keator Prud'homme

*Dr. James Elias Keator M.D.
(1822-1908) grandfather of Lucile
Keator Prud'homme*

Mayo, Kenneth and Al III with wagon, 1933

Full name:	*James Alphonse Prud'homme, III*
Wife:	*Martha Jane Allen*
Death:	*June 13, 1988*
Children:	*James Alphonse Prud'homme, IV*

1st Wife: Sandra Lee

2nd Wife: Mary Ellen Donovan
Children: James Alphonse Prud'homme, V
            Christopher Prud'homme

Sandra Lynn Prud'homme (twin)

1st Husband: Joe Beck Payne
Children: Michael Dylan Payne
            Scott Allen Payne

2nd Husband: G. Michael Haynie, M.D.
Stepchildren: John Marshall Haynie
               Caroline King Haynie
               Clare Elise Haynie

Kathy Jane Prud'homme (twin)
Husband: Terry Guin
Renee Elise Prud'homme
Husband: Antonio Quiros
Children: Zachary Allen Quiros
Michael Allen Prud'homme
Wife: Verina Lisa Ochoa
Child: Victoria "Tori" Lynn Prud'homme
Stepchild: Dylan Williams

Lucile K. Prud'homme in 1992 with children and grandchildren of Alphonse III:
L to R: Renee Quiros, Jamie (Alphonse V), Alphonse IV, Christopher Prud'homme, Lucile,
Dylan Payne, Scott Payne, Kathy Guin, Sandra Prud'homme (Haynie),
Michael Prud'homme. Courtesy Guillet Photography

Dylan Payne, Sandra P. Haynie, Marshall Haynie, Mike Haynie, Caroline Haynie, Scott Payne, Clare Haynie at Oakland, 1996 Courtesy Guillet Photography

Zachary Quiros, son of Renee Prud'homme Quiros, playing on the porch at the store, circa 1999 Courtesy Guillet Photography

Full name:	Kenneth Andrew Prud'homme
Wife:	Sally Anne Calhoun
Children:	Catherine Adeline Prud'homme
	Anne Lucille Prud'homme

Husband: Francisco Aviles
Children: Hannah Francis Aviles
Sarah Catherine Aviles
Kenneth Andrew "Drew" Prud'homme

Sarah and Hannah Aviles in their grandfather's chair,
heirloom from Oakland

Home of Mr. and Mrs. Kenneth Prud'homme, photo taken in 1920s before restoration. Architectural historians believe the home was built about 1798-1800. The earliest French documentation found reveals Athanasse Poissot and Bouvard St. Amant, owned the land in 1839 wherein reference is made to a home.

Full name:	*Mayo Keator Prud'homme*
Wife:	*Annette Berry*
Children:	*Julie Michelle Prud'homme (twin)*
	Husband: Yanni Demartinos
	Children: Annette Athena Demartinos
	Mayo "Tad" Keator Prud'homme, Jr. (twin)
	Wife: Judith
	Children: Megan Harpe
	Ashley Hunter

Mayo, Jr. and Julie Prud'homme on the gallery of Oakland, 1965

Full name:	Rose Vivian Prud'homme
1st Husband:	Eugene Joseph Flores
Children:	Andrea Minette Flores

Full name: *Rose Vivian Prud'homme*
1st Husband: *Eugene Joseph Flores*
Children: *Andrea Minette Flores*
                            Husband: Christopher Shaw Winder
                            Children: Amanda Winder
                                            Bridgett Winder
                        Eugene Joseph Flores, Jr.
                        Denise Annette Flores
                            Husband: Kenneth Lawton Poleman
                            Children: Lawton Poleman
                                Keator Poleman
                                Collin Poleman

2nd Husband: *Ted Edward Duggan*
            Stepchildren: *Ted Edward Duggan, Jr.*
                        Samuel Reed Duggan
                        Kelle Ann Duggan Nugent
                        Janice Ann Duggan Brewer
                        Monica Lyn Duggan Wisenbaker
                        Gregory Cade Duggan
                        Julie Ellen Duggan Kuehler

*Benjamin Metoyer
townhouse, Natchitoches*

The Duggan —Flores family at Viv and Ted's marriage (Feb. 1999)
Front Row: Greg Duggan, Sam Duggan, Ted Duggan, Sr., Ted Duggan, Jr .and
Eugene Flores. Back Row: Julie D. Kuehler, Monica D. Wisenbaker, Janice D.
Brewer, Vivian Prud'homme Flores Duggan, Denise F. Poleman, Andrea
F. Winder and Kelle D. Nugent

About the Artist

Irma Sompayrac Willard was one of the most delightful ladies to ever enrich the lives of many along Cane River. Raised on Willow Plantation near Grand Ecore, Louisiana, "Miss Irma" was educated at St. Mary's Academy, Louisiana State Normal School (now Northwestern State University in Natchitoches, La.) and at Sophie-Newcomb College in New Orleans while receiving her degree in Fine Arts from Tulane. She also studied at the Art Students League in New York, the American University in Washington, the Webster School of Art at Cape Cod, and in France. She received her Masters degree in art and art education from Columbia University.

Miss Irma married David Willard in the 1920's and they had one son, Daniel. She continued to study art as well as history throughout her multiple trips to Europe. Being a direct descendant of Jean Pierre Phillipe Prud'homme, the first Prud'homme to live in the Louisiana territory, Miss Irma visited the homes of her ancestors while in France. Miss Irma's great-great grandfather was Antoine Prud'homme, brother to Emmanuel, builder of Oakland Plantation.

Irma Sompayrac Willard

Front Cover: The original artwork of Oakland (presented on the cover) was sketched by Ms Irma and given to Kathy Prud'homme and Terry Guin as a wedding gift in 1977.

About the Author

Sandra Prud'homme Haynie, better known as "Sam" was raised on a farm on Cane River in Bermuda, Louisiana. Her father and uncle farmed Oakland Plantation. She is a graduate of Northwestern State University in Natchitoches, Louisiana and Paul M. Hebert Law School, Louisiana State University in Baton Rouge. She currently practices law with the firm of Rountree, Cox, Guin and Achee in Shreveport, La.

Sources

Battles and Leaders of the Civil War, Castle, a division of Book Sales, Inc. Secaucus, N.J.

Baudier, Roger Sr. K.S.G. The Catholic Church in North Louisiana. Compiled at the direction of His Excellency, The Most Reverend Charles Pascal Greco, D.D., Sixth Bishop of the Diocese of Alexandria, in commemoration of the Centennial of the Diocese, May 1953.

Breedlove, Caroline, Bermuda/Oakland Plantation, 1830-1880. Graduate School of Northwestern State University of Louisiana. 1999

Brock, Eric J. Eric Brock's Shreveport. Pelican Publishing Co. Gretna, La. 2001

Brown, Dee. The American Spa: Hot Springs, Arkansas Rose Publishing Company, Little Rock, Arkansas 1982

Cammie Henry Research Center, Northwestern State University, Natchitoches, La

Cardin, Clifton. Images of America: Bossier Parish, Arcadia, Charleston, S.C. 1999

Center for African and African-American Studies, University of Texas at Austin

Conrad, Glenn R. A Dictionary of Louisiana Biography, The Louisiana Historical Association in cooperation with The Center for Louisiana Studies of the University of Southwestern Louisiana, New Orleans 1988.

DeBlieux, Robert B. A Driving Tour Down Cane River and through Kisatchie National Forest. The Natchitoches Times, 1993.

DeBlieux, Robert B. Natchitoches: A Walking Tour of the Historic District. The Natchitoches, Times, 1989.

De Villiers du Terrage, Marc. The Last Years of French Louisiana, Center for Louisiana Studies, University of Southwestern Louisiana, Lafayette, La. 1982

Dollar, Susan E. Oaklawn Plantation, History 4040, Northwestern State University, 1990.

Fortier, Alcee. <u>Louisiana</u>. Volume III, Biographical, Atlanta: Southern Historical Association 1909.

Estes, Craig A. <u>Natchitoches</u>, Baton Rouge Bureau for Lath and Plaster Grant, Louisiana State University, Baton Rouge, La. 1969

Giraud, Marcel. <u>A History of French Louisiana, Volume Five, The Company of the Indies, 1723-1731.</u> Louisiana State University Press, 1987

Gore, Laura Locoul, <u>Memories of the Old Plantation Home & A Creole Family Album</u>. The Zoe Company, Inc., Vacherie, La. 2000

Irma Sompayrac Willard Collection. Lestan Prudhomme diary. Cammie Henry Research Center, Eugene P. Watson Memorial Library, Northwestern State University of Louisiana. Original in Howard-Tilton Memorial Library, Tulane University, New Orleans.

Leavitt, Mel. <u>A Short History of New Orleans</u>. San Francisco, LEXIKOS, 1982

Malone, Ann Patton, Ph.D. <u>Oakland Plantation, Its People's Testimony</u>. Report for the Naional Park Service, 1998.

McCall, Edith, <u>Conquering the Rivers: Henry Miller Shreve and the Navigation of America's Inland Waterways.</u> Louisiana State University Press, Baton Rouge and London. 1984

McCants. Sister Dorothea Olga. Daughters of the Cross. <u>With Valor They Serve: A Sequel to They Came To Louisiana</u> Baton Rouge, Louisiana, Claitor's Publishing Division. 1975.

Miller, Christina and Susan E. Wood, <u>Oakland Plantation: A Comprehensive Subsurface Investigation.</u> Cane River National Historical Park, Natchitoches Parish, Louisiana, Southeast Archcological Center, National Park Service, Tallahassee, Florida, 2000.

Mills, Gary B. <u>The Forgotten People: Cane River's Creoles of Color.</u> Baton Rouge: Louisiana State University Press. 1977.

Natchitoches Genealogical and Historical Association, Old Courthouse Building, Second Street, Natchitoches, Louisiana

Nardini, Louis Raphael Sr. <u>My Historic Natchitoches, Louisiana And Its Environment.</u> Colfax, La. Colfax Printing Co. 1963

Noel Memorial Library, Archives and Special Collections of Louisiana State University in Shreveport, Coll 354, St. Vincent's Academy.

Phares, Ross, <u>Cavalier in the Wilderness</u> Louisiana State University Press, Baton Rouge, La., 1952

Prud'homme, Lucile Keator and Fern Christensen. <u>Natchitoches Cemeteries.</u> New Orleans: Polyanthos, Inc., 1977.

Prud'homme Family Papers, Southern Historical Collection, Wilson Library, University of North Carolina at Chapel Hill.

Robert DeBlieux Collection, Cammie Henry Research Center, Eugene P. Watson Memorial Library, Northwestern State University of Louisiana.

Saxon, Lyle. <u>Old Louisiana.</u> Pelican Publishing Co. Gretna, La 1998.

Seebold, Herman de Bachelle, M.D. <u>Old Louisiana Plantation Homes and Family Trees</u> Pelican Publishing Co., Gretna 1941.

Stacey, Truman. <u>Louisiana's French Heritage.</u> Acadian House Publishing, Lafayette, Louisiana, 1990

Stallings, Evelyn Tudor. <u>Cane River Physician: The Practice and Letters of Dr. J. A. Leveque, 1832-1893.</u> M.A. candidate, Northwestern State University, 1987

University of Notre Dame Archives, Hesburgh Library, Notre Dame, Indiana

Wells, Carol. <u>Cane River Country Louisiana.</u> Northwestern State University Press, Natchitoches, La. 1979.